MASTERS OF ART

# GIOTTO AND MEDIEVAL ART

The lives and works of the medieval artists

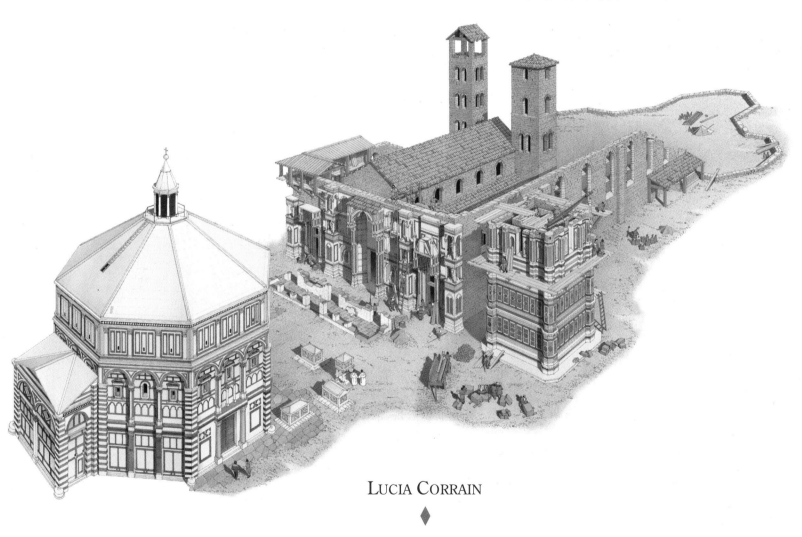

LUCIA CORRAIN

◆

ILLUSTRATED BY
SERGIO
*with the assistance of*
ANDREA RICCIARDI

**MACDONALD YOUNG BOOKS**

# DoGi

Produced by
*Donati Giudici Associati, Florence*
Original title:
*Giotto e l'arte nel Medioevo*
Text:
*Lucia Corrain*
Illustrations:
*Sergio*
*Andrea Ricciardi*
Picture research and
coordination of co-editions:
*Caroline Godard*
Art direction:
*Oliviero Ciriaci*
Page design:
*Sebastiano Ranchetti*
Editing:
*Enza Fontana*
English translation:
*Simon Knight*
Editor, English-language edition:
*Ruth Nason*
Typesetting:
*Ken Alston – A.J. Latham Ltd*

© 1995 Donati Giudici Associati s.r.l.
Florence, Italy
English language text © 1995 by
Macdonald Young Books/
Peter Bedrick Books
First published in Great Britain
in 1995 by
Macdonald Young Books
Campus 400
Maylands Avenue
Hemel Hempstead
Herts HP2 7EZ

ISBN 0 7500 1677 9

A catalogue record for this book is
available from the British Library.

Printed in Italy by Amilcare Pizzi,
Cinisello Balsamo, Milan

Photolitho:
Mani, Florence

# ◆ HOW THE INFORMATION IS PRESENTED

*Every double-page spread is a chapter in its own right, devoted to an aspect of the life and art of Giotto or the major artistic and cultural developments of his time. The text at the top of the left-hand page (1) and the central illustration are concerned with this main theme. The text in italics (2) gives a chronological account of events in Giotto's life. The other material (photographs, paintings and drawings) enlarges on the central theme.*

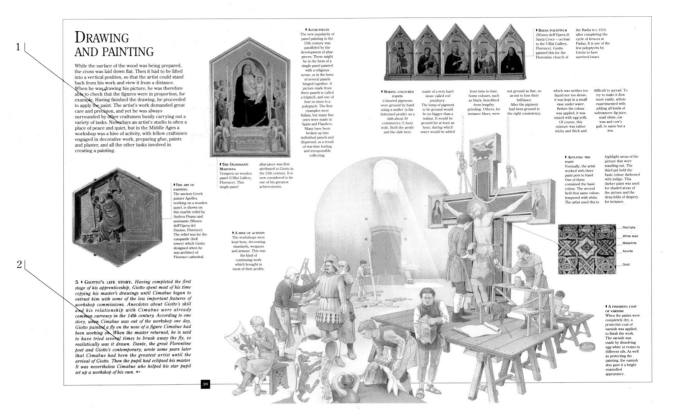

1

2

*Some pages focus on the works of art created by Giotto, in particular his great fresco cycles depicting the lives of St Francis of Assisi, Joachim and Anna, Mary and Jesus. These are presented complete, or nearly so. The various episodes are arranged in succession, rather like cartoon strips, so that they can be interpreted according to the original intentions of the artist and his assistants. The double page reproduced below shows the first few episodes in the life of St Francis.*

## THE STORY OF ST FRANCIS

It was common for artists in the Middle Ages to paint a series of panels representing progressive scenes in a story. A famous cycle of frescos of this kind, depicting the life of St Francis at Assisi, adorns the walls of the Upper Church of St Francis at Assisi. The cycle consists of twenty-eight panels around the lower part of the walls of the nave and entrance. They are arranged three to each window bay, with the exception of the first bay from the main door, which contains four panels. In the entrance, there is one scene on the wall on either side of the main door. Each panel representing an individual episode is framed by painted cornices and by painted barley-sugar columns left and right. The succession of events shown in the fresco cycle follows the story of the saint as set out in St Bonaventure's *Greater Life of St Francis*, written between 1260 and 1263. Giotto worked on the fresco cycle between 1290 and 1296. It is unlikely that he worked on his own, as the frescos vary in quality and some of the painting is not of the highest standard. It seems very likely that Giotto was responsible for the overall design and for the preparatory drawings, with a large team of helpers involved in the actual painting.

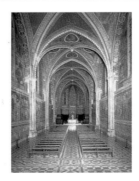

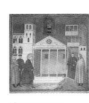

**1. THE HOMAGE OF A SIMPLE MAN**

**2. FRANCIS AND THE POOR KNIGHT**

**3. THE DREAM OF THE PALACE**

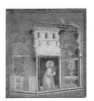

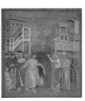

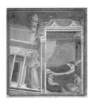

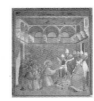

**4. THE MIRACLE OF THE CRUCIFIX**

**5. FRANCIS RENOUNCES HIS EARTHLY POSSESSIONS**

**6. THE DREAM OF INNOCENT III**

**7. CONFIRMATION OF THE RULE**

**8. THE VISION OF THE FLAMING CHARIOT**

**9. THE VISION OF THE THRONES**

# CONTENTS

# CONTEMPORARIES

In the late 13th and early 14th centuries, Europe was experiencing a period of unprecedented growth. The population was steadily increasing, trade flourished, cities were expanding, and new churches and civic buildings were going up everywhere. Central Italy at this time was the scene of a renewal in Western art, of which the outstanding figure was Giotto di Bondone. He was a pupil of Cimabue and worked with major sculptors and painters including Arnolfo di Cambio, Duccio di Buoninsegna, Pietro Cavallini and Simone Martini. Giotto worked for popes and kings, and especially for the new religious orders which had sprung up in the 13th century, the Franciscans and Dominicans. After centuries of Byzantine influence, the figures painted by Giotto were people of flesh and blood, depicted in familiar settings.

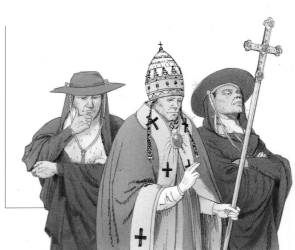

**NICHOLAS IV ♦**
The first Franciscan pope (1288-92). He was the instigator of some important fresco cycles.

**BONIFACE VIII ♦**
(c.1235-1303) He became pope in 1294, and commissioned some major works of art from Giotto.

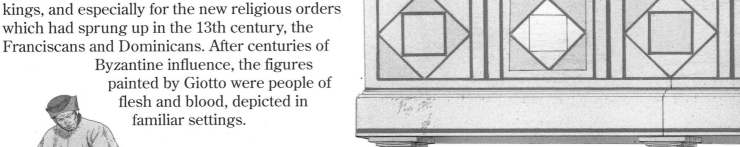

**ARNOLFO DI CAMBIO ♦**
The best-known architect and sculptor of his day, he was born at Colle di Val d'Elsa in c.1245 and died in Florence in 1302.

**MASO DI BANCO ♦**
Born in Florence in the latter part of the 13th century, he was a pupil of Giotto and is considered one of his worthiest successors.

**DANTE ♦**
(1265-1321) Born in Florence in the same year as Giotto, he is considered the greatest of Italian poets, and father of the Italian language. His chief work is the *Divine Comedy*.

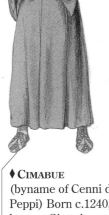

**♦ CIMABUE**
(byname of Cenni di Peppi) Born c.1240, he was Giotto's teacher and the greatest painter of the preceding generation. He died sometime after 1302.

**GIOTTO ♦**
(c.1267-1337) Born at Colle di Vespignano, Giotto di Bondone was responsible for a renewal in painting, depicting human figures, landscapes and buildings in a more realistic way than previous artists. He died in Florence.

**TADDEO GADDI ♦**
He worked for twenty-four years in Giotto's workshop (1313-37). After Giotto's death, he became one of the most famous Florentine painters.

**BERNARDO DADDI ♦**
Born in Florence in the late 13th century, he was a pupil of Giotto. He died in 1348.

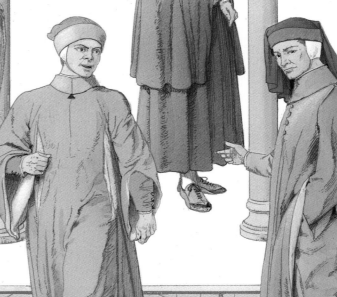

**A LABOURER ♦**
Labourers were paid to perform various menial tasks in the master's workshop.

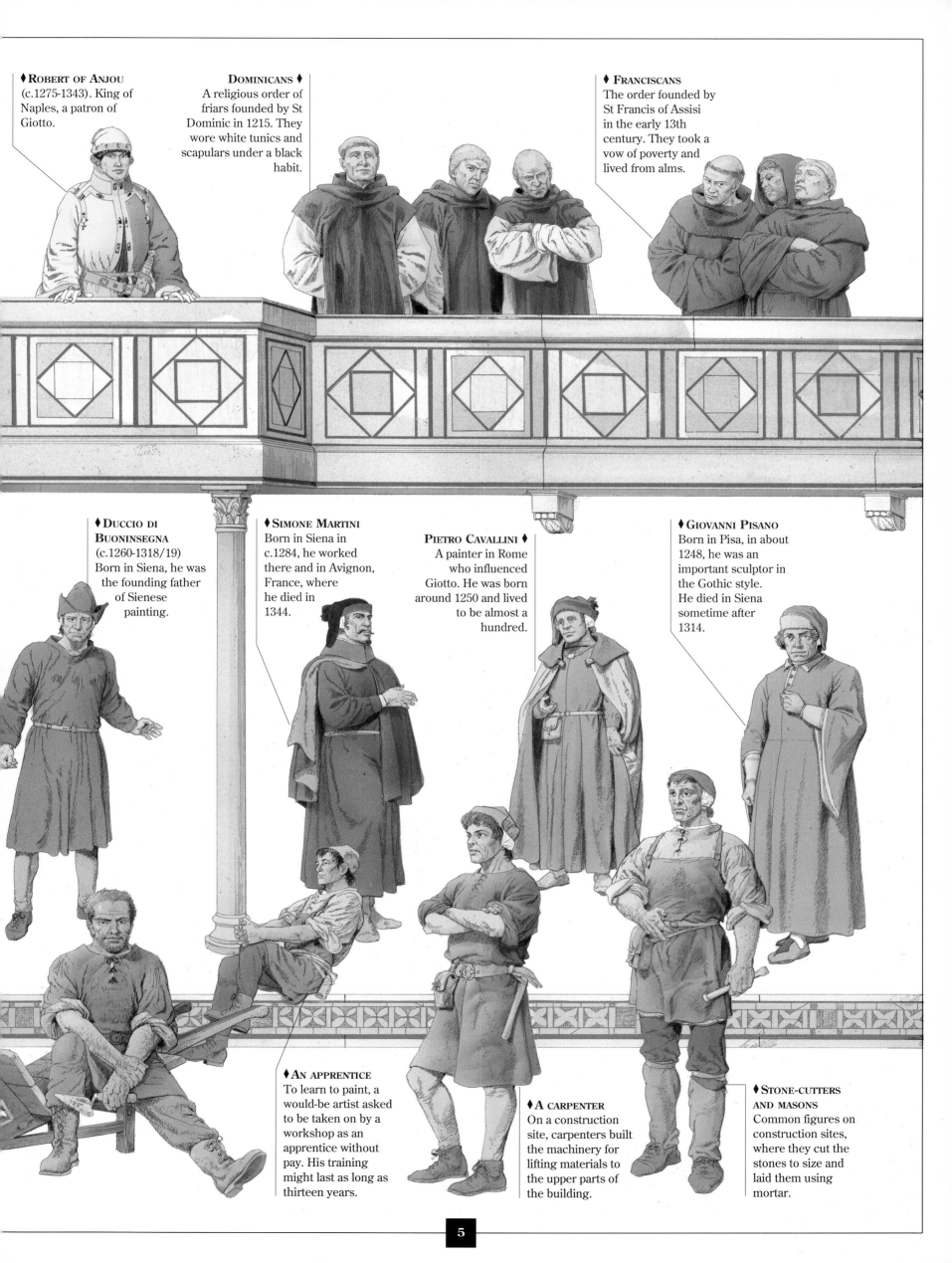

♦ **ROBERT OF ANJOU** (c.1275-1343). King of Naples, a patron of Giotto.

**DOMINICANS** ♦ A religious order of friars founded by St Dominic in 1215. They wore white tunics and scapulars under a black habit.

♦ **FRANCISCANS** The order founded by St Francis of Assisi in the early 13th century. They took a vow of poverty and lived from alms.

♦ **DUCCIO DI BUONINSEGNA** (c.1260-1318/19) Born in Siena, he was the founding father of Sienese painting.

♦ **SIMONE MARTINI** Born in Siena in c.1284, he worked there and in Avignon, France, where he died in 1344.

**PIETRO CAVALLINI** ♦ A painter in Rome who influenced Giotto. He was born around 1250 and lived to be almost a hundred.

♦ **GIOVANNI PISANO** Born in Pisa, in about 1248, he was an important sculptor in the Gothic style. He died in Siena sometime after 1314.

♦ **AN APPRENTICE** To learn to paint, a would-be artist asked to be taken on by a workshop as an apprentice without pay. His training might last as long as thirteen years.

♦ **A CARPENTER** On a construction site, carpenters built the machinery for lifting materials to the upper parts of the building.

♦ **STONE-CUTTERS AND MASONS** Common figures on construction sites, where they cut the stones to size and laid them using mortar.

# RELIGIOUS ART IN THE MIDDLE AGES

Over the centuries, artists in the Western tradition chose to paint and sculpt scenes from history and mythology and everyday life, but, most of all, they worked on religious subjects. The earliest examples of Christian art in the West are in the catacombs of Rome and North Africa. From AD 313, when the Roman Emperor Constantine legalized Christian worship, the Old Testament, the Gospels and the lives of saints and martyrs became the main source of subjects for European art for over a thousand years. The early Christians feared that putting statues in holy places might lead to a revival of pagan idol worship. Then, in the 6th century, Pope Gregory the Great encouraged the display of religious paintings as a way of teaching the Christian faith to people who could not read and write. The religious art of the 6th to the 12th centuries was in the Byzantine style, so called after Byzantium, the ancient name of Constantinople. This city was the capital of the eastern part of the Roman Empire.

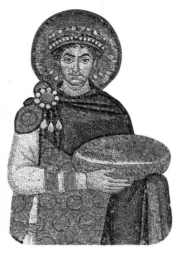

**♦ EMPEROR JUSTINIAN**
A detail from a 6th-century mosaic, in the church of San Vitale, Ravenna.

**♦ THE BYZANTINE EMPIRE**
In AD 476, when the western part of the Roman Empire fell to the Barbarians, the eastern part survived for another thousand years. It became known as Byzantium or the Byzantine Empire, and its capital was Constantinople, founded by Emperor Constantine in AD 300. Throughout the Middle Ages, the Empire waxed and waned until Constantinople was finally conquered by the Turks in 1453. The Empire reached its height under Justinian, Emperor from 527 to 565. The city of Ravenna became the seat of Byzantine power in Italy. It is in the north-east of the country. Ravenna became the centre of a brilliant civilization, from which Byzantine culture spread to Rome and throughout northern Italy. The Byzantine tradition in art predominated until the 12th century. Artists represented Christian subjects and their paintings and mosaics were meant to be instructive, to produce feelings of awe and take the spectator's mind off human things. Therefore they did not try to show things in a realistic way.

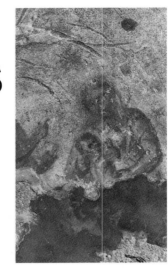

**♦ PAINTING IN THE CATACOMBS**
*Mary with the child Jesus*, a fragment of a 3rd-century mural painting, Catacomb of Priscilla, Rome.

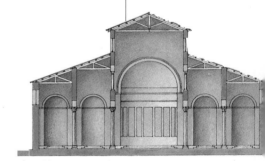

**♦ A CHRISTIAN BASILICA**
The building consists of a wide central nave, separated from the narrower side aisles by two rows of columns. At the end of the nave is a semi-circular structure known as the apse.

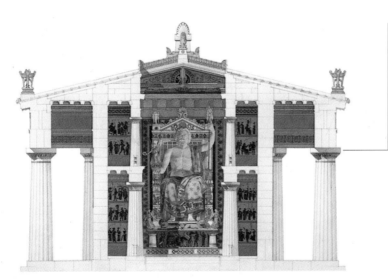

**♦ TEMPLES**
Classical temples were relatively small, as they were designed to house a statue of the god or goddess to whom they were dedicated, and religious ceremonies normally took place outside. The spread of Christianity initiated a new phase in the history of religious architecture.

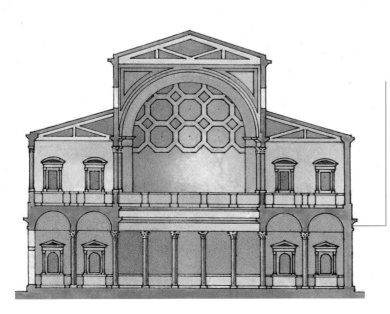

**♦ A ROMAN BASILICA**
The new Christian churches were built to a plan which resembled that of large ancient Roman buildings known as basilicas. The Romans had built these as palaces or as halls to use as courts of law or covered markets or for holding public meetings.

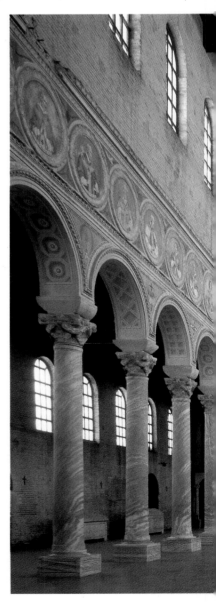

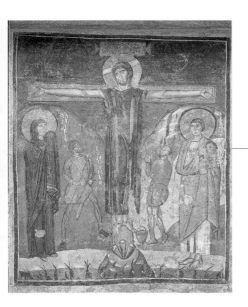

♦ **CRUCIFIXION**
Chapel of Saints Quirico and Giulitta, Santa Maria Antiqua, Rome, 741-752. This is one of the very few crucifixions in which Christ on the cross is shown as alive and dressed in priestly garments. The picture was to explain that the Church and its priests represented Christ on earth.

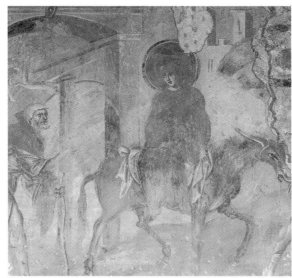

♦ **THE ROAD TO BETHLEHEM**
Santa Maria Foris Portas, Castelseprio. This fresco cycle was painted by an artist of great talent, though we know neither his name nor where he came from. Its exact age is also unknown. It was painted between the 6th and the 8th centuries AD.

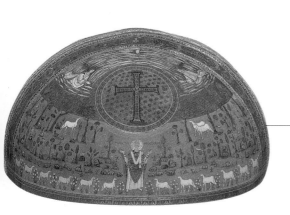

♦ **SANT'APOLLINARE IN CLASSE**
The building that is closest in form to the early Christian basilicas, despite changes made to it over the centuries, is the church of Sant'Apollinare in Classe, near Ravenna. Left: a detail from the 6th-century mosaic which decorates the apse.

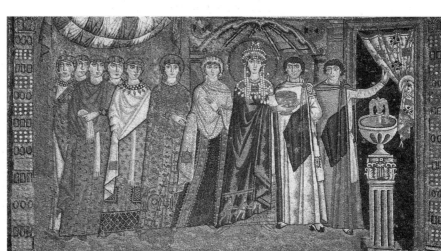

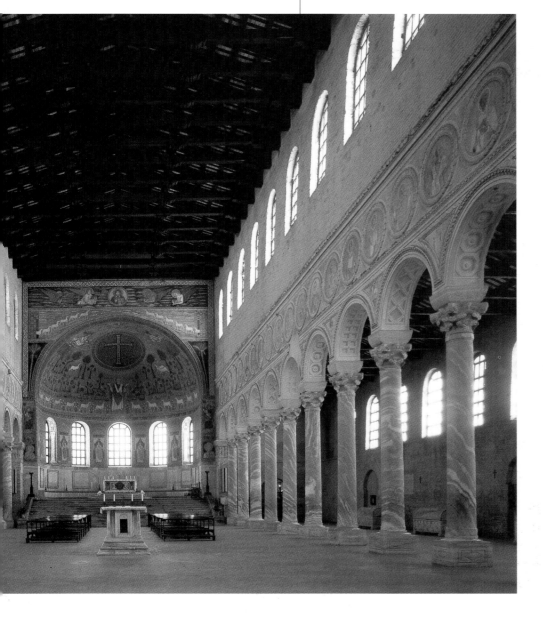

♦ **CHARACTERISTICS OF BYZANTINE ART**
The figures in Byzantine mosaics are unlike those in earlier, classical Roman art. The most important difference is that the Byzantine artists did not attempt to imitate reality. Their scenes have no depth and there is no definite light source. Because there is no shadow, the figures appear flat. They are isolated and static. Mosaics, laboriously formed from small pieces (tesserae) of coloured stone or glass, covered the whole interior of a church. The light reflecting from them gave a sense of intense warmth. Above: *The Empress Theodora and her court*, San Vitale, Ravenna, mid-6th century.

**FORMAL DECORATION** ♦
Byzantine churches were decorated in a formalized, hierarchical way, as we see here in the cathedral of Monreale, c.1190. In the upper part of the apse, Christ is depicted as Pantocrator (ruler of the universe, in the act of giving his blessing). Below him is the Virgin Mary and, lower still, figures of prophets, apostles, martyrs and saints.

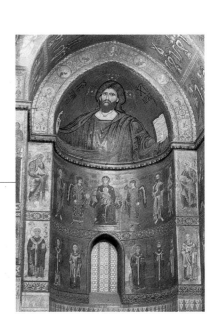

# CHURCHES AND CATHEDRALS

After the year 1000, Europe went through a ferment of change, as new religious buildings went up in towns and villages. Economic progress was paralleled by developments in styles of art. In little more than two hundred years, the Christian West was swept first by the Romanesque style and then by the Gothic style of architecture. The new religious orders, such as the Dominicans and Franciscans, paid for churches and religious houses to be built in or on the outskirts of towns, and people living in towns themselves financed the construction of great cathedrals. The building sites of the period were centres of experimentation in technology, engineering and architecture. The new buildings also gave scope to painters and sculptors to exercise their decorative talents. The photographs show cathedrals and churches built in Britain, France, Germany, Italy and Spain.

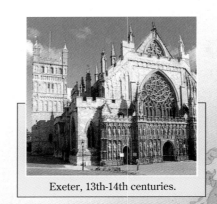
Exeter, 13th-14th centuries.

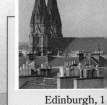
Edinburgh, 1

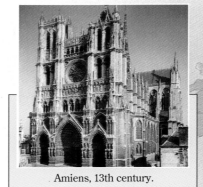
Amiens, 13th century.

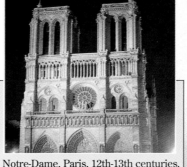
Notre-Dame, Paris, 12th-13th centuries.

Map labels: Edinburgh, Durham, York, Westminster, Exeter, Salisbury, London, Canterbury, Amiens, Caen, Reims, Mont-St-Michel, Paris, Chartres, Tours, Autun, Cluny, Arles, Santiago de Compostela, León, Pamplona, Salamanca, Burgos, Ávila, Ripoll, Córdoba, Granada

**♦ A BUILDING SITE** Work on a building site tended to continue for many years, and often for several generations. One reason for building taking so long was that building work followed the rhythm of the seasons. Another was that only animal power was available to drag blocks of stone from the quarries, and so this process was slow. Below: An illustration of a building site, showing pulleys, scaffolding and stone-cutters' tools, from *Grandes Chroniques de Saint Denis*, 14th century.

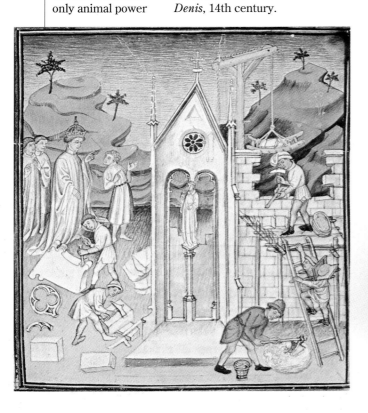

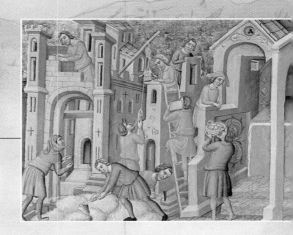

**CATHEDRALS ♦** Cathedrals are called by that name because they contain the bishop's *cathedra* or throne. They were built with money donated by the faithful, who were granted indulgences in return. Right: from the 13th-century Canterbury Psalter (Bibliothèque Nationale, Paris).

Burgos, 13th century.

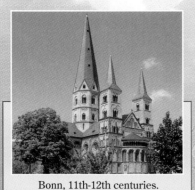
Bonn, 11th-12th centuries.

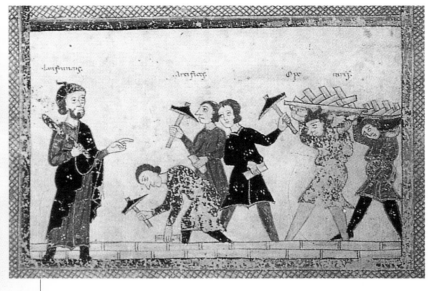

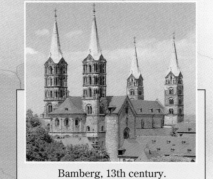
Bamberg, 13th century.

Magdeburg

Prague

Bamberg

Regensburg

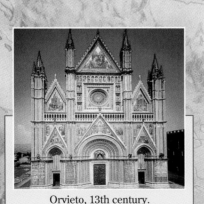
Assisi, 13th century.

• Torcello

• Parma
• Modena
• Bologna

Pistoia
cca •
Pisa • Florence
Siena

• Assisi
• Orvieto

Trani

Naples

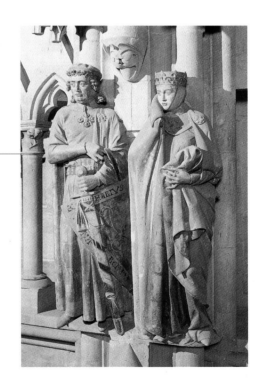
Orvieto, 13th century.

• Monreale

**♦ THE ARCHITECT**
The architect Lanfranco, as depicted in the 13th-century *Relatio Translationis corpori sancti Geminiani*, Capitoline Library, Modena. The architect had overall responsibility for the building project, but he was assisted by many other skilled craftsmen, including stone-dressers, masons and plasterers. The job of the carpenters was to build machinery for moving building materials and hoisting finished decorative pieces of stonework to their final locations on the upper parts of the building.

**ECKHARDT AND UTA ♦**
These statues of about 1260 are in the west choir of Naumburg cathedral in Germany. The sculptor at Naumburg was commissioned to portray the cathedral's founders and so he created realistic figures modelled on actual individuals.

**♦ ROMANESQUE AND GOTHIC**
New churches and great cathedrals were built in towns and villages throughout Europe between the 11th and 13th centuries. Shown on the map are the main places where important churches were built in the Romanesque and Gothic styles.

**STAINED GLASS ♦**
Part of a stained-glass window representing the stone-masons, at Bourges cathedral, 12th century. The art of glass-making developed mainly in France and in the Germanic north.

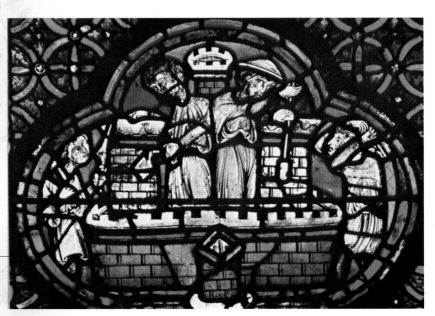

# SCULPTURE BEFORE THE TIME OF GIOTTO

Sculptors were particularly active on cathedral building sites in the Middle Ages. Decorating the outside of the cathedral, they worked especially on the main door and the area around it, where their reliefs were most likely to be seen. Inside, they carved the capitals of columns and pilasters, the pulpit and other elements which would be in full view of the worshippers. Sculpture became a way of communicating the Christian faith to people who could not read, and so religious buildings came to be seen as great illustrated books. In the 13th century, the best sculptors came from France, which was the richest and most powerful country in Europe. Their work was imitated by German and English masters. In Italy, sculpture began to flourish towards the end of the 13th century, particularly in the workshops of Nicola and Giovanni Pisano and Arnolfo di Cambio.

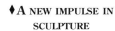

♦ **A NEW IMPULSE IN SCULPTURE**
Nicola Pisano worked for many years in Pisa, which was then a great port at the mouth of the river Arno. Following the example of the French masters, he began studying ancient Roman sculpture, which influenced the way he portrayed human figures and animals.

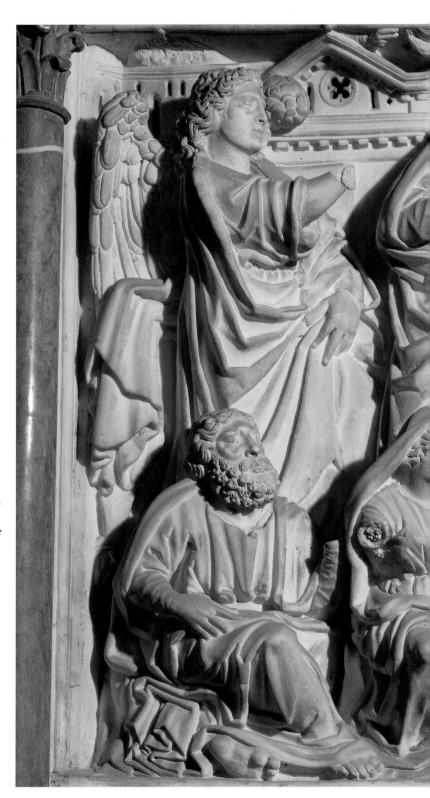

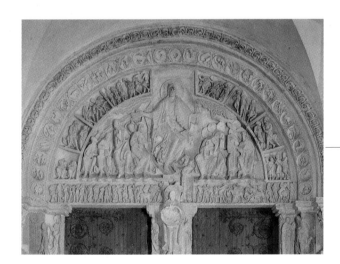

♦ **VÉZELAY**
Lunette over the main door of the church of La Madelaine, Vézelay, 1135-c.1140. The sculpture represents the sending out of Christ's apostles, the descent of the Holy Spirit and Christ's ascension into heaven.

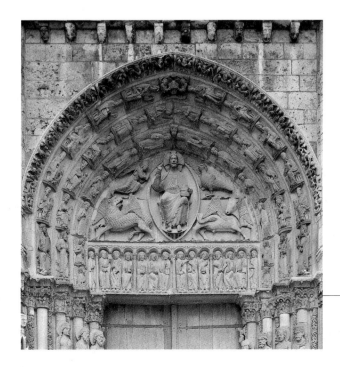

♦ **CHARTRES**
Lunette over the west door of the cathedral, 1145-55. Christ in glory is sculpted on the tympanum. The twelve apostles are represented on the lintel below.

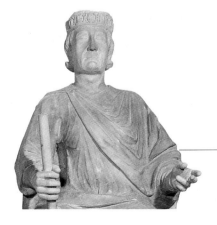

♦ **CHARLES OF ANJOU**
Capitoline Museum, Rome, 1277. Attributed to Arnolfo di Cambio, this was one of the first sculptures since ancient times to be a true portrait.

♦**THE NATIVITY AND THE ANNUNCIATION TO THE SHEPHERDS** A detail from the marble pulpit which Nicola Pisano carved for the Baptistery at Pisa, finishing in 1260.

Following medieval tradition, Pisano represented more than one episode in the same panel, a practice known as continuous representation.

The Madonna is reclining on a bed of straw and Joseph huddles in the left-hand corner, while two women are busy bathing the new-born Jesus. The flock of sheep beside the women, turning towards the right, belong to the scene that is depicted in the top right of the panel: the angels announcing the news of the birth of Jesus to the shepherds. The panel includes realistic details. For example, there is a figure of a goat scratching its head with its hoof.

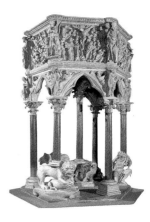

♦**PULPIT**
Giovanni Pisano, Sant'Andrea, Pistoia, 1298-1308.

♦**NICOLA PISANO**
Nicola is thought to have been born around 1220 and to have trained in his native Puglia (the heel of Italy). He later worked in Pisa and Siena. Referring back to classical Roman sculpture, he sought to portray the human figure in a natural, realistic way.

♦**GIOVANNI PISANO**
Nicola's son Giovanni was born in Pisa in about 1248 and died in Siena c.1314-19. He worked with and learned from his father but developed his own style of sculpture, incorporating European Gothic influences. He sculpted the façade of Siena cathedral and pulpits at Pistoia and Pisa. His works convey great human feeling.

♦**ARNOLFO DI CAMBIO**
(1245-1302)
Arnolfo was Nicola Pisano's pupil, then became his associate. As an architect, he was one of the first to harmonize architectural and sculptural elements. Compared with his master, he gave more emphasis to the rational, classical aspect of his art.

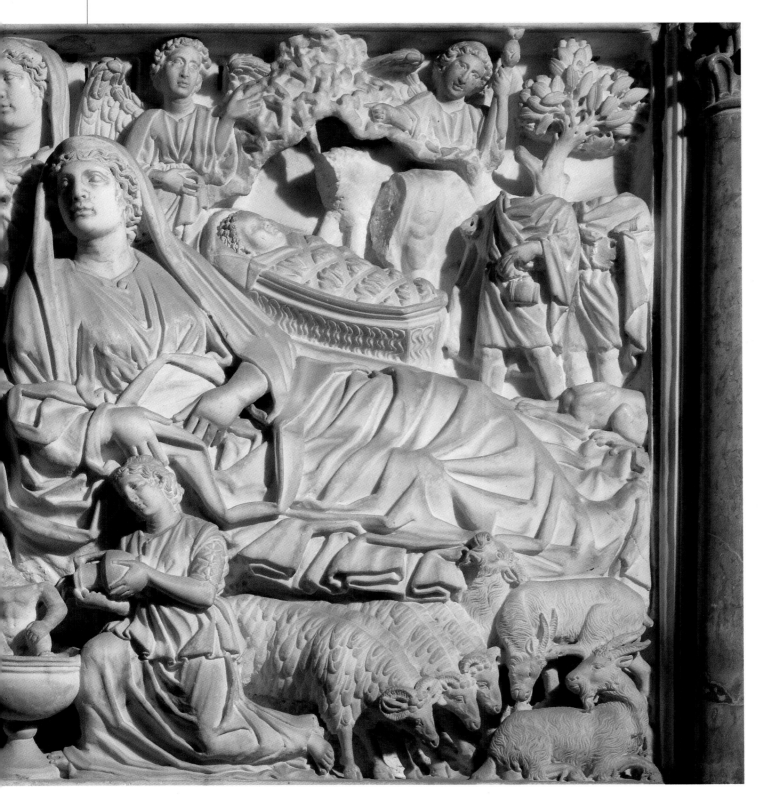

**DORMITIO VIRGINIS** ♦
This means the falling asleep, i.e. death, of the Virgin Mary. A marble sculpture by Arnolfo di Cambio, 1302, for the façade of Florence cathedral (Staatliche Museen, Berlin).

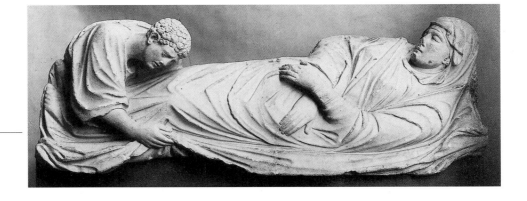

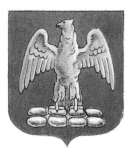

♦ THE GUILD OF
MERCHANTS, OR THE
CALIMALA

♦ THE GUILD SYSTEM
The economic and
political life of
Florence was
regulated by its
guilds. These were
associations of
merchants who were
all engaged in the
same or related
activities. Each guild
had its headquarters
and coat of arms. The
guilds laid down rules
on work permits,
apprenticeships and
qualifications for full
membership.
Through the guilds,
the merchant classes
controlled the city
government.
Magistrates were
elected at first from
the members of the
Calimala, and of the
wool and money-
changers' guilds. The
system was then
expanded to include
the silk merchants,
physicians and
apothecaries,
furriers, and finally
the judges and
notaries. These were
the seven major
guilds.

# FLORENCE IN THE 13TH CENTURY

The Tuscan city of Florence, in the heart of Italy, had been on a par with neighbouring towns such as Pisa, Siena and Lucca, but, in the 13th century, it came to the fore as one of Europe's major centres of commerce, textile manufacture and banking. In 1252, the Florentines began minting a gold coin, the florin, which became Europe's most important and reliable medium of foreign exchange. By the end of the century, the population of Florence had grown to 100,000, and so the city ranked with Paris, London and Milan. The rapid expansion of Florence was accompanied by the building of churches and town houses. In the second half of the century, the city resembled a huge building site. Florence had long been split between warring factions and torn by intense political rivalries, but during the 13th century a new ruling class of textile manufacturers, merchants and bankers emerged. By establishing the Ordinances of Justice, in 1293, they introduced a more stable form of government, which lasted for many years.

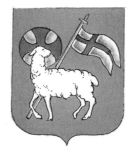

♦ THE WOOL GUILD

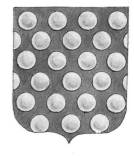

♦ THE GUILD OF
MONEY-CHANGERS

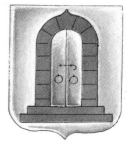

♦ THE GUILD OF SILK
MERCHANTS

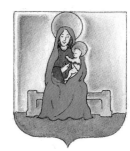

♦ THE GUILD OF
PHYSICIANS AND
APOTHECARIES

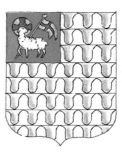

♦ THE GUILD OF
FURRIERS

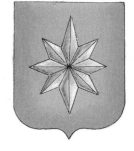

♦ THE GUILD OF
JUDGES AND
NOTARIES

♦ TOWERS
From a distance, on account of its many high towers, Florence had the appearance of a fine, prosperous city. In fact, the towers reflected the feuds within the city.

When one faction came to power, it demolished the towers of its rivals, and built more towers of its own. This happened repeatedly, as the fortunes of different families changed.

Sometimes several families banded together to build a tower. They all had access to the tower from their own homes, so that they could take refuge there in times of danger.

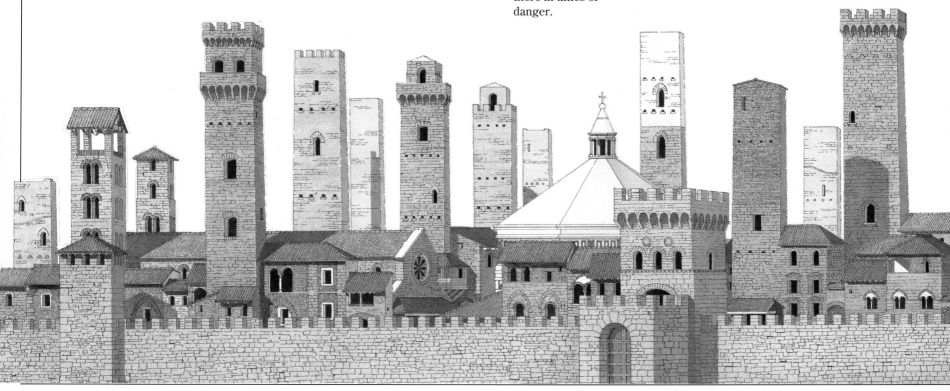

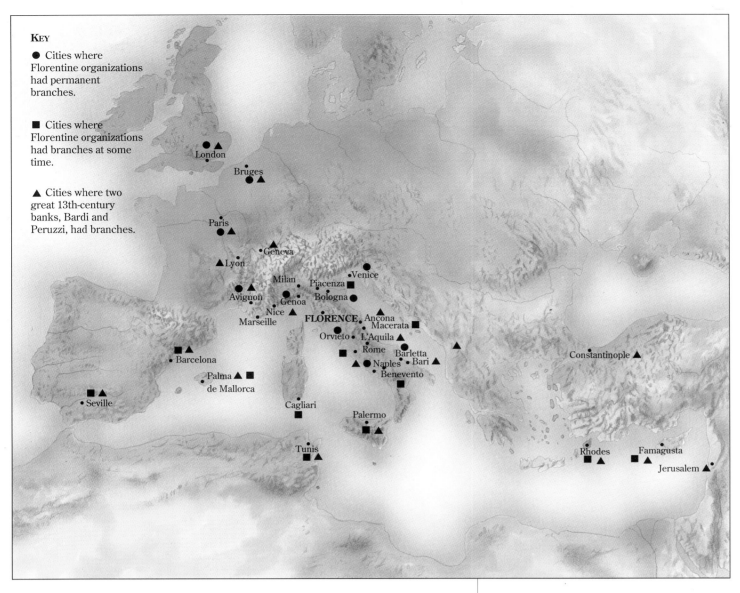

KEY

● Cities where Florentine organizations had permanent branches.

■ Cities where Florentine organizations had branches at some time.

▲ Cities where two great 13th-century banks, Bardi and Peruzzi, had branches.

London
Bruges
Paris
Geneva
Lyon
Milan
Piacenza
Venice
Avignon
Genoa
Bologna
Nice
FLORENCE
Ancona
Marseille
Macerata
Orvieto
L'Aquila
Rome
Barletta
Barcelona
Naples
Bari
Benevento
Palma de Mallorca
Constantinople
Seville
Cagliari
Palermo
Rhodes
Famagusta
Tunis
Jerusalem

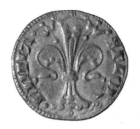

♦ THE GOLD FLORIN
The mid-13th century saw an important development in the history of Western money: gold coins of a standard weight and content were minted. The first examples were the Genoese genovino, the Florentine florin (1252) and, later, the Venetian ducat (1284). The gold florin had a lily stamped on one side. It was an absolutely dependable currency, which was accepted in international transactions. In this way, it held a rather similar position in the medieval financial world as the pound or the dollar do today.

♦ FOREIGN TRADE
Florentine merchants and bankers also operated abroad. Their commercial organizations and banks had branches in the major European cities. Their agents lent money, purchased raw materials and arranged for the import of goods that had been made in Florence.

At times in the 11th and 12th centuries, there were as many as a hundred and fifty such towers.

Between 1250 and 1258, a limit was imposed on the height to which towers could be built.

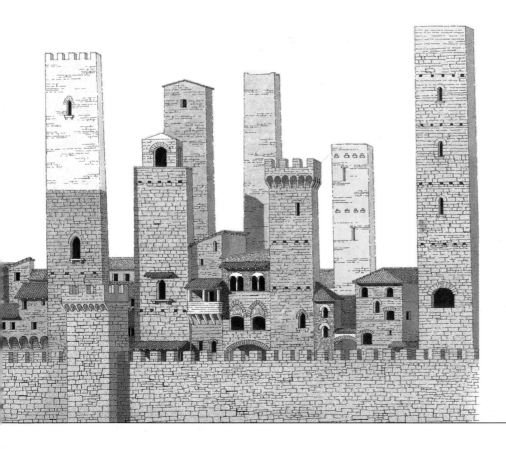

## GIOTTO'S LIFE STORY

**1 ♦** *In the Middle Ages, painters and sculptors, who often also practised as architects, decorators and goldsmiths, were regarded simply as craftsmen. Of no great social standing, they belonged to the mechanical guilds. Important commissions alternated with mundane tasks such as decorating furniture, saddles or armour. Little is known of most artists; signed works are rare. Some of the earliest examples are the mosaics of Saint Denis in France (1140) and the stained glass windows of Chartres cathedral, which incorporate small self-portraits of their authors. Not until the second half of the 13th century did artists begin to enjoy greater prestige. Giotto is one of the first artists about whom chroniclers recorded significant factual information. This was due also to the fact that he came from the proud and powerful city of Florence, whose rulers wanted to record its history for posterity.* ≫→

# CIMABUE, GIOTTO'S TEACHER

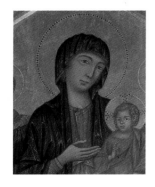

♦ ENTHRONED
MADONNA WITH CHILD
A detail from a painting
by Cimabue, 1285-86
(Uffizi Gallery,
Florence).

♦ CIMABUE
Born in Florence
between 1240 and
1245, Cimabue is
considered the
greatest painter of the
generation preceding
Giotto. He evidently
felt a need to free
himself from
Byzantine
conventions and paint
in a new style. He
may also have been
influenced by the new
forms of sculpture he
saw in Rome and
Pisa. At Assisi, he
worked with Giotto
and Duccio di
Buoninsegna, on two
*Crucifixions* in the
basilica of St Francis
(1278-79). In Bologna
he worked at Santa
Maria dei Servi; in
Florence, on the vault
of the Baptistery; and
in Pisa, on the mosaic
of St John in the apse
of the cathedral. His
paintings on wood
include *Crucifixions* at
Arezzo and in Santa
Croce in Florence,
and the *Maestà* now
displayed in the
Uffizi.

In the centre of Florence stands the building known as
the Baptistery of St John, where Florentines are
traditionally baptized. Built in the 11th century, it is
rigorously geometrical in structure. The mosaics
inside the vault show clearly how artists changed the
way in which they represented the real world during
the course of the 13th century. There is a huge
difference between the mosaics begun in 1225 and
those from the last quarter of the century, particularly
in regard to the human figures. It is evident that, in
Florence, changes in art went hand in hand with
economic and social development. In the late 13th
century, the best-known and most admired painter in
Italy was a Florentine, Cenni di Peppi, known as
Cimabue. He revived the art of painting, departing
from the Byzantine style to show people and things in
a more realistic way.

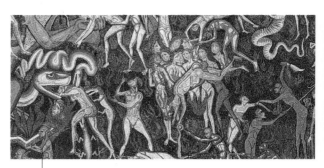

♦ A LATER EXAMPLE
A mosaic representing
hell, believed to be the
work of Coppo di
Marcovaldo, a Tuscan
artist of the second
half of the 13th
century. The artist has
obviously tried to
escape from
Byzantine rigidity by
using bold outlines
and strong contrasts
of dark and light.

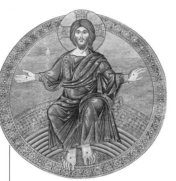

♦ A MOSAIC OF 1225
This early 13th-
century mosaic of
*Christ pantocrator*
was made for the
Baptistery by the
workshop of Meliore.
The static quality of
the figure and the lack
of any illusion of depth
are typical of the
Byzantine tradition.

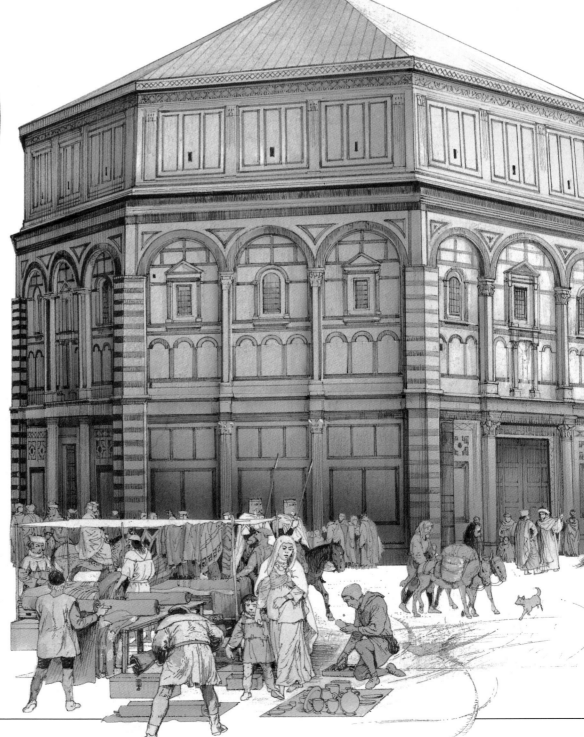

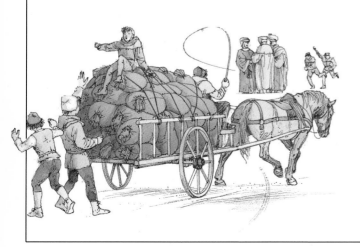

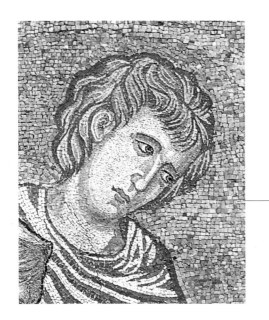

**♦ THE FACE OF AN ONLOOKER**
A detail from *The Naming of John the Baptist*, a mosaic at the Baptistery. This was made between 1270 and 1272 by an artist in Cimabue's circle. The face of the bystander is highly expressive, and the sense of movement conveyed by the whole figure is unlike anything in Byzantine art.

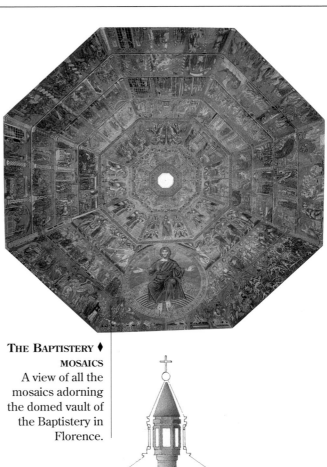

**THE BAPTISTERY ♦ MOSAICS**
A view of all the mosaics adorning the domed vault of the Baptistery in Florence.

**THE DANCE ♦ OF SALOME**
The figures have been given volume, and the room in which they are shown seems to have real depth. This mosaic in the Baptistery is by the workshop of an unknown master, whom art historians call the Magdalene Master.

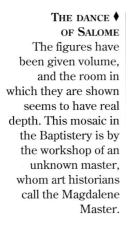
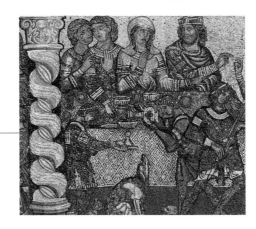

**♦ THE LOWERING OF CHRIST'S BODY**
A mosaic by the workshop of the Magdalene Master. Distress is conveyed by the expressions on the faces of the disciples and by the gestures people are making. Mary Magdalene, on the extreme left, raises her arms in despair.

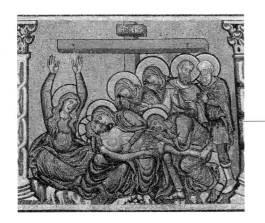

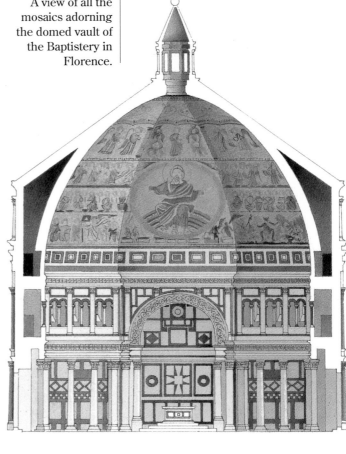

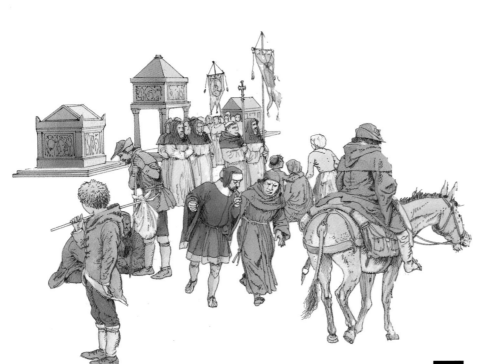

**2 ♦ GIOTTO'S LIFE STORY.** *The name Giotto is probably a shortened form of Angiolotto, Angelo or Biagio. Giotto was born at Colle di Vespignano, in the Mugello area north of Florence, in 1267. His father, Bondone, grew crops and raised sheep. Early chroniclers have handed down a curious legend. One day, at the age of ten, while looking after the sheep, Giotto was drawing one of them with a sharp stone on a flat piece of rock. Cimabue, the great painter of the time, happened to be passing that way and, surprised by the boy's ability, persuaded his father to let him join him in his workshop. The reality is somewhat different. It is a known fact that, during Giotto's boyhood, many country people were leaving the land and moving into Florence. Bondone was one of them. In the Tuscan capital, he first sent his son to work for the wool guild. Then, aware of his talents, he placed him in Cimabue's workshop.* ⟫

# THE WORKSHOP

Although some artists had made a name for themselves, painting was not a particularly prestigious occupation in 13th-century Florence. It tended to attract the sons of less well-to-do families, because the apprenticeship fees were lower than in other trades. A boy who wanted to become a painter had to be taken on by a workshop. This was where the master made his home, as well as carrying on his trade. The workshop also served as a shop: the wares for sale were displayed to passers-by under the wide arches that separated the ground floor rooms from the street. So the workshop was a big, roomy building. When a new apprentice was engaged, a contract was drawn up in the presence of a notary and witnesses. The contract stipulated that the boy must live in the workshop and that the master must teach him his trade. Whether or not the apprentice was paid depended on the particular case. An apprenticeship might last anything from four to thirteen years. The apprentice first learned to prepare canvases and paints, and was then introduced to the art of drawing and, finally, to the skills of painting.

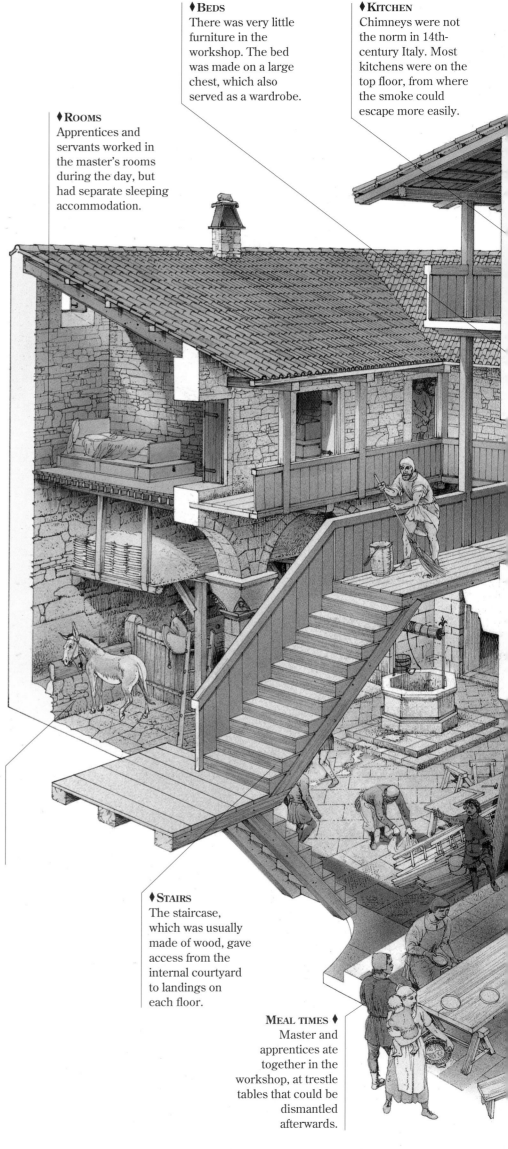

♦ **BEDS**
There was very little furniture in the workshop. The bed was made on a large chest, which also served as a wardrobe.

♦ **KITCHEN**
Chimneys were not the norm in 14th-century Italy. Most kitchens were on the top floor, from where the smoke could escape more easily.

♦ **ROOMS**
Apprentices and servants worked in the master's rooms during the day, but had separate sleeping accommodation.

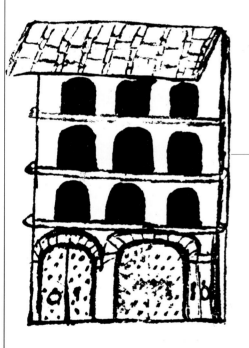

♦ **LIVING ABOVE THE SHOP**
A drawing of a typical Florentine house in the early years of the 14th century. The main door and workshop are on the ground floor, the living quarters above.

**STABLE** ♦
Every house had a stable, usually to house a donkey, which was the most common form of transport.

♦ **STAIRS**
The staircase, which was usually made of wood, gave access from the internal courtyard to landings on each floor.

**MEAL TIMES** ♦
Master and apprentices ate together in the workshop, at trestle tables that could be dismantled afterwards.

**3 ♦ GIOTTO'S LIFE STORY.** *Giotto must have shown early signs of promise, because the workshop that took him on was the best-known in Florence. Cimabue ran this workshop, with a number of assistants to help him meet the requirements of his local customers. In addition, his work was much in demand in other Italian cities, in particular Pisa, Rome, Assisi and Arezzo. Although still bound to a considerable extent by the Byzantine tradition, Cimabue was an innovator in representing human facial expressions. The young Giotto had fallen on his feet: he accompanied Cimabue on his long trips to Rome and Assisi.* ≫♦

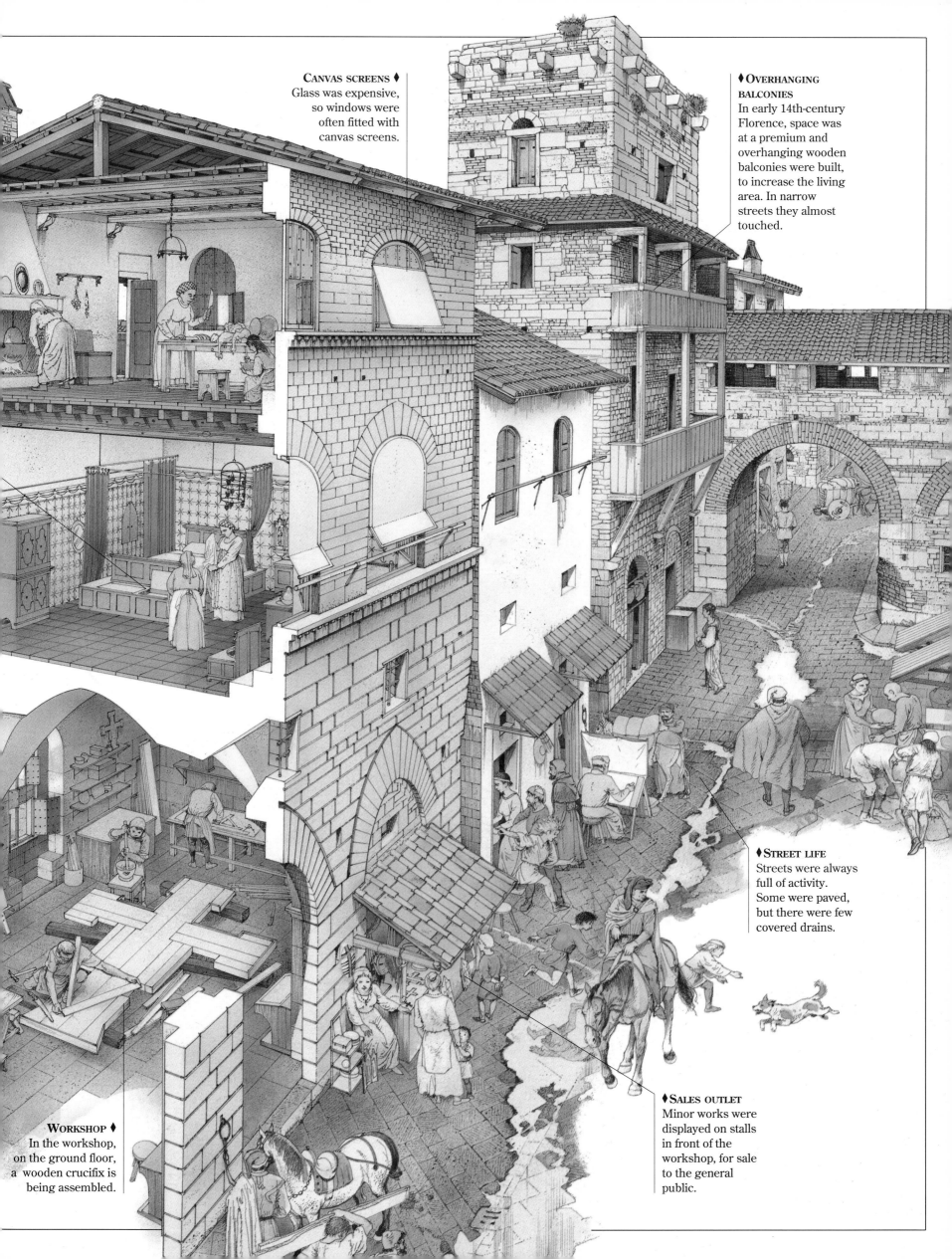

**CANVAS SCREENS ◆**
Glass was expensive, so windows were often fitted with canvas screens.

**◆ OVERHANGING BALCONIES**
In early 14th-century Florence, space was at a premium and overhanging wooden balconies were built, to increase the living area. In narrow streets they almost touched.

**◆ STREET LIFE**
Streets were always full of activity. Some were paved, but there were few covered drains.

**◆ SALES OUTLET**
Minor works were displayed on stalls in front of the workshop, for sale to the general public.

**WORKSHOP ◆**
In the workshop, on the ground floor, a wooden crucifix is being assembled.

# PAINTING ON PANELS

The practice of painting on wooden panels goes back to ancient times. In Egypt, this technique was known as early as the 13th or 12th century BC, and historians believe it was also practised by the Greeks and Romans. However, in Europe, miniature and mural painting were the prevailing forms until the early years of the 13th century AD. After that time, painting on panels became more widespread and popular. The Italian painter Cennino Cennini (c.1370-c.1440) wrote a book called *Il Libro dell'Arte (The Craftsman's Handbook)*, in which he described what artists of his time had to do to prepare a panel for painting. Great care had to be taken to coat the wood with several layers of a material that gave a smooth surface. The surface also needed to be elastic, so that it would not crack, but would expand and contract with the wood underneath it.

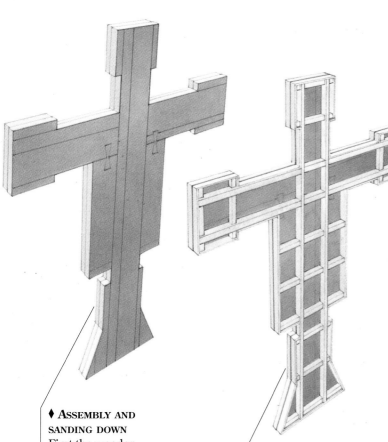

♦ **ASSEMBLY AND SANDING DOWN**
First the wooden planks were assembled into the desired shape – for instance, a cross. Then the wood was cleaned and planed smooth. Any knots were removed and the holes were filled with a mixture of glue and sawdust.

♦ **TREATING THE BACK**
The back of the cross was covered with a mixture of paint and linseed oil, to make the wood waterproof and give it an even appearance. The finished cross was to be free-standing, and so would be visible from behind.

♦ **PREPARATION**
The careful work of preparing a large wooden panel before the painting began was carried out in several stages. It was necessary to leave some days between one stage and the next.

**1. SIZING** ♦
A soft, broad brush was used to cover the entire surface and frame with three coats of glue. This made the wood water-resistant.

**2. COVERING WITH** ♦ **CLOTH**
The next stage was to stick strips of thin canvas soaked in glue to the cross and its frame. It was important to avoid overlapping.

**4. SMOOTHING THE** ♦ **SURFACE**
To give the gesso a compact surface, it was scraped lightly with a sharp blade. The aim was to achieve a glossy, ivory-like finish.

**8. GILDING** ♦
The craftsman polished the areas that had been coated in bole with an animal tooth, and then applied the gold or silver leaf. He used tweezers to pick up one of the ultra-thin sheets of metal and position it on the bole. To fix it in its final position, he pressed it with a piece of cotton wadding.

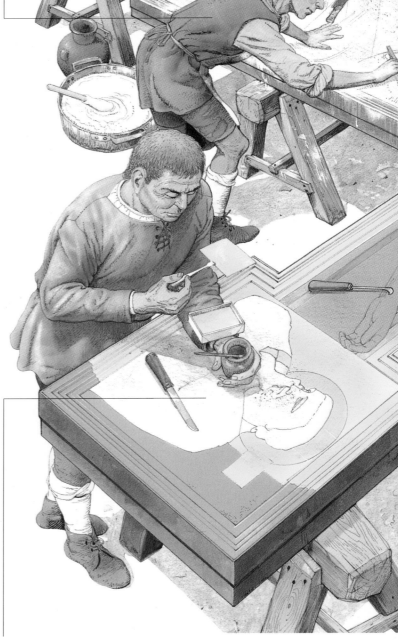

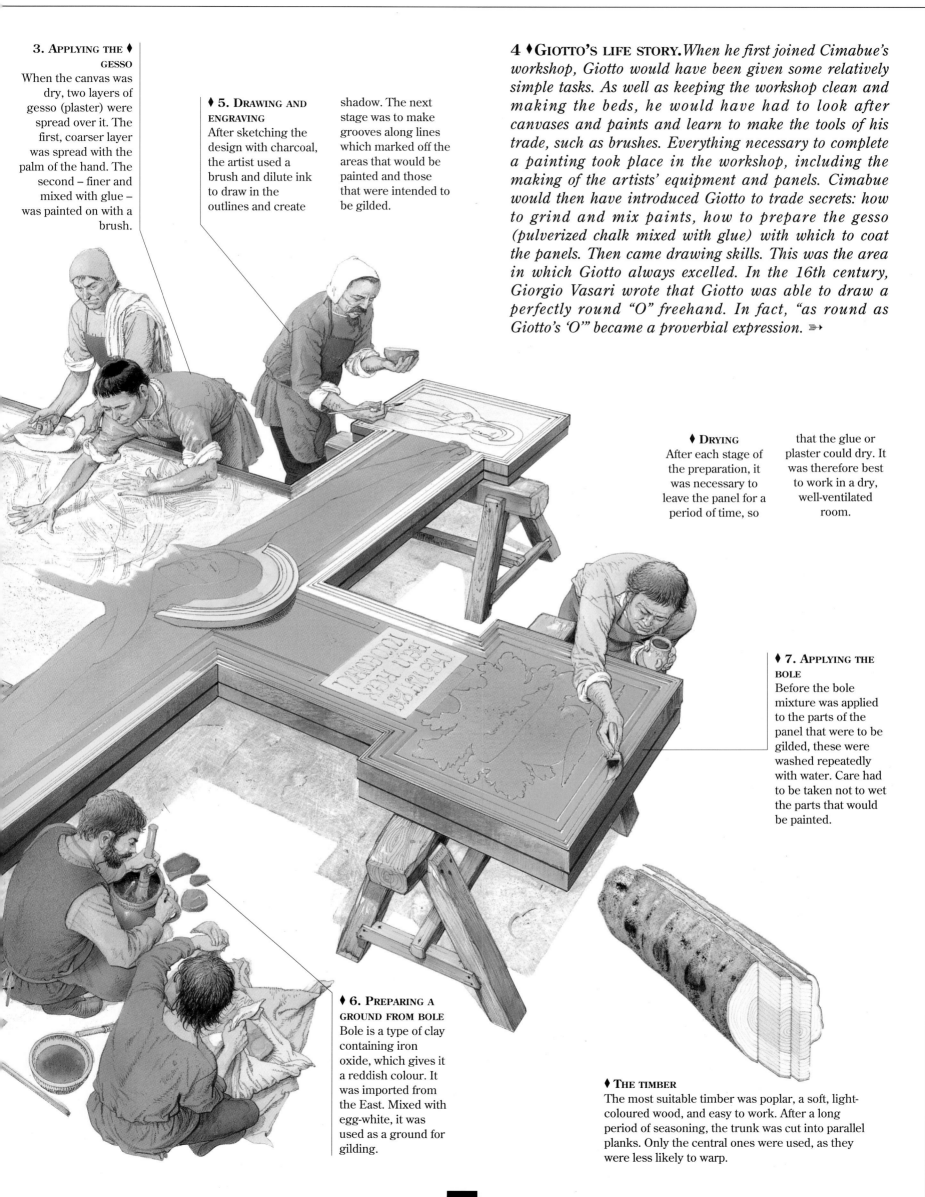

**3. APPLYING THE ♦ GESSO**
When the canvas was dry, two layers of gesso (plaster) were spread over it. The first, coarser layer was spread with the palm of the hand. The second – finer and mixed with glue – was painted on with a brush.

**♦ 5. DRAWING AND ENGRAVING**
After sketching the design with charcoal, the artist used a brush and dilute ink to draw in the outlines and create shadow. The next stage was to make grooves along lines which marked off the areas that would be painted and those that were intended to be gilded.

**4 ♦ GIOTTO'S LIFE STORY.** *When he first joined Cimabue's workshop, Giotto would have been given some relatively simple tasks. As well as keeping the workshop clean and making the beds, he would have had to look after canvases and paints and learn to make the tools of his trade, such as brushes. Everything necessary to complete a painting took place in the workshop, including the making of the artists' equipment and panels. Cimabue would then have introduced Giotto to trade secrets: how to grind and mix paints, how to prepare the gesso (pulverized chalk mixed with glue) with which to coat the panels. Then came drawing skills. This was the area in which Giotto always excelled. In the 16th century, Giorgio Vasari wrote that Giotto was able to draw a perfectly round "O" freehand. In fact, "as round as Giotto's 'O'" became a proverbial expression.* ≫▸

**♦ DRYING**
After each stage of the preparation, it was necessary to leave the panel for a period of time, so that the glue or plaster could dry. It was therefore best to work in a dry, well-ventilated room.

**♦ 7. APPLYING THE BOLE**
Before the bole mixture was applied to the parts of the panel that were to be gilded, these were washed repeatedly with water. Care had to be taken not to wet the parts that would be painted.

**♦ 6. PREPARING A GROUND FROM BOLE**
Bole is a type of clay containing iron oxide, which gives it a reddish colour. It was imported from the East. Mixed with egg-white, it was used as a ground for gilding.

**♦ THE TIMBER**
The most suitable timber was poplar, a soft, light-coloured wood, and easy to work. After a long period of seasoning, the trunk was cut into parallel planks. Only the central ones were used, as they were less likely to warp.

# DRAWING AND PAINTING

While the surface of the wood was being prepared, the cross was laid down flat. Then it had to be lifted into a vertical position, so that the artist could stand back from his work and view it from a distance. When he was drawing his picture, he was therefore able to check that the figures were in proportion, for example. Having finished the drawing, he proceeded to apply the paint. The artist's work demanded great care and precision, and yet he was always surrounded by other craftsmen busily carrying out a variety of tasks. Nowadays an artist's studio is often a place of peace and quiet, but in the Middle Ages a workshop was a hive of activity, with fellow craftsmen engaged in decorative work, preparing glue, paints and plaster, and all the other tasks involved in creating a painting.

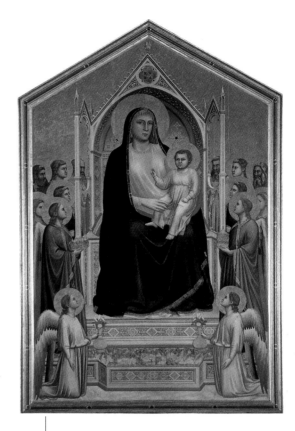

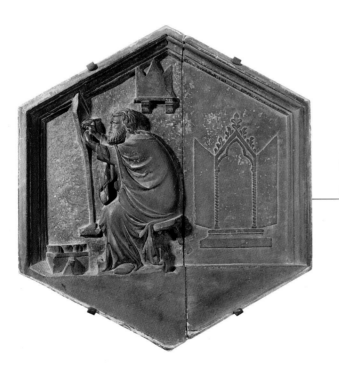

♦ **THE ART OF PAINTING**
The ancient Greek painter Apelles, working on a wooden panel, is shown on this marble relief by Andrea Pisano and assistants (Museo dell'Opera del Duomo, Florence). The relief was for the campanile (bell tower) which Giotto designed when he was architect of Florence cathedral.

♦ **THE OGNISSANTI MADONNA**
Tempera on wooden panel (Uffizi Gallery, Florence). This single-panel altar-piece was first attributed to Giotto in the 15th century. It is now considered to be one of his greatest achievements.

♦ **ALTAR-PIECES**
The new popularity of panel painting in the 13th century was paralleled by the development of altar-pieces. These might be in the form of a single panel painted with a religious scene, or in the form of several panels hinged together. A picture made from three panels is called a triptych, and one of four or more is a polyptych. The first examples were Italian, but many fine ones were made in Spain and Flanders. Many have been broken up into individual panels and dispersed, as a result of war-time looting and irresponsible collecting.

♦ **A HIVE OF ACTIVITY**
The workshops were kept busy, decorating standards, weapons and armour. This was the kind of continuing work which brought in most of their profits.

**5** ♦ **GIOTTO'S LIFE STORY.** *Having completed the first stage of his apprenticeship, Giotto spent most of his time copying his master's drawings until Cimabue began to entrust him with some of the less important features of workshop commissions. Anecdotes about Giotto's skill and his relationship with Cimabue were already common currency in the 14th century. According to one story, when Cimabue was out of the workshop one day, Giotto painted a fly on the nose of a figure Cimabue had been working on. When the master returned, he is said to have tried several times to brush away the fly, so realistically was it drawn. Dante, the great Florentine poet and Giotto's contemporary, wrote some years later that Cimabue had been the greatest artist until the arrival of Giotto. Then the pupil had eclipsed his master. It was nevertheless Cimabue who helped his star pupil set up a workshop of his own.* ➤

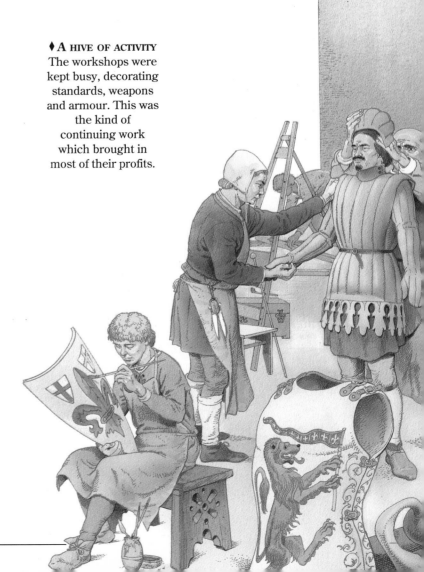

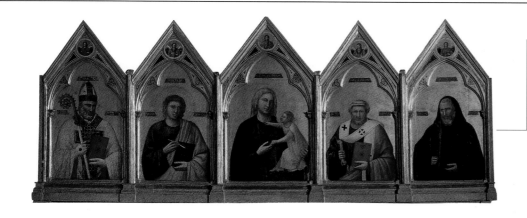

♦ **BADIA POLYPTYCH**
(Museo dell'Opera di Santa Croce – on loan to the Uffizi Gallery, Florence). Giotto painted this for the Florentine church of the Badia in c.1310, after completing the cycle of frescos at Padua. It is one of the few polyptychs by Giotto to have survived intact.

♦ **MAKING COLOURED PAINTS**
Coloured pigments were ground by hand using a muller (a flat-bottomed pestle) on a slab about 30 centimetres (1 foot) wide. Both the pestle and the slab were made of a very hard stone called red porphyry.
The lump of pigment to be ground would be no bigger than a walnut. It would be ground for at least an hour, during which water would be added from time to time. Some colours, such as black, benefitted from lengthy grinding. Others, for instance blues, were not ground so fine, so as not to lose their brilliance.
After the pigment had been ground to the right consistency, which was neither too liquid nor too dense, it was kept in a small vase under water. Before the colour was applied, it was mixed with egg yolk. Of course, this mixture was rather sticky and thick and difficult to spread. To try to make it flow more easily, artists experimented with adding all kinds of substances: fig juice, snail slime, ear wax and cow's gall, to name but a few.

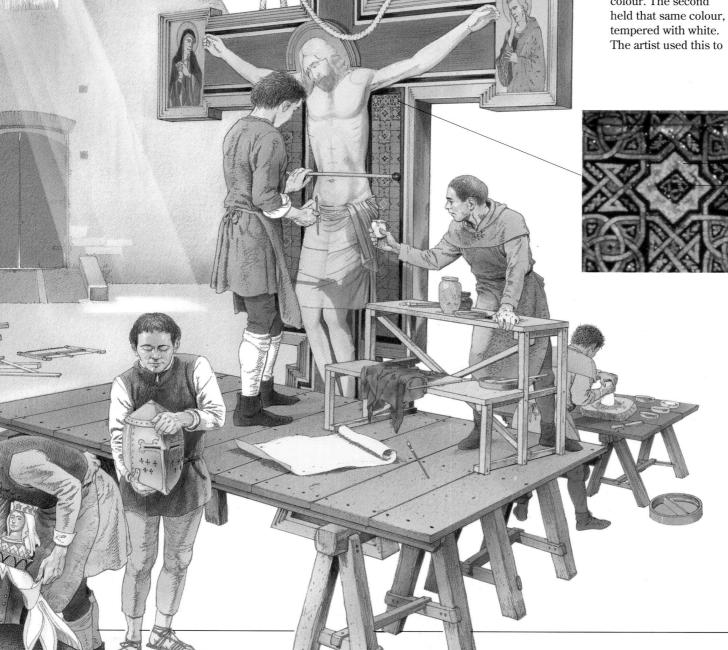

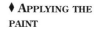

♦ **APPLYING THE PAINT**
Normally, the artist worked with three paint pots to hand. One of them contained the basic colour. The second held that same colour, tempered with white. The artist used this to highlight areas of the picture that were standing out. The third pot held the basic colour darkened with indigo. This darker paint was used for shaded areas of the picture and the deep folds of drapery, for instance.

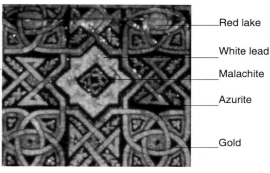

Red lake

White lead

Malachite

Azurite

Gold

♦ **A FINISHING COAT OF VARNISH**
When the paints were completely dry, a protective coat of varnish was applied, to finish the work. The varnish was made by dissolving egg white or resins in different oils. As well as protecting the painting, the varnish also gave it a bright enamelled appearance.

# THE DOMINICANS

♦ DOMINGO DE GUZMÁN

St Dominic was born around 1170 at Caleruega in Spain. As a young student, he was known for the simple life he led and his compassion for the poor. As a priest, he was sent to preach against the Albigensian heretics in the south of France. In 1215, in Toulouse, he founded the religious Order of Friars Preachers, which subsequently became a mendicant order (one that lives by begging for alms). He died in Bologna in 1221.

In earlier centuries, when men joined a religious order such as the Benedictines or the Cluniacs, this meant that they separated themselves from the world to lead a life of work, prayer and study in the confines of their monasteries. New religious orders which grew up rapidly in the 13th century were different. Their members, known as friars, lived in direct contact with the secular society around them. They adopted a life of poverty, depending on the generosity of the faithful to bring them what they needed to survive. The Dominican order was founded by Domingo de Guzmán in 1215, and its way of life included begging for alms and preaching. The order often attracted men of considerable intellect, and was also known as the Order of Friars Preachers or Black Friars.

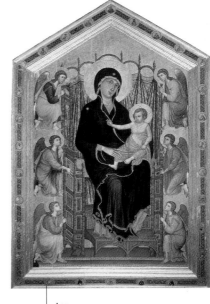

♦ DUCCIO DI BUONINSEGNA

This *Maestà* of 1285 (Uffizi Gallery, Florence) is known as the *Rucellai Madonna*. It is an altar-piece commissioned for one of the chapels of Santa Maria Novella.

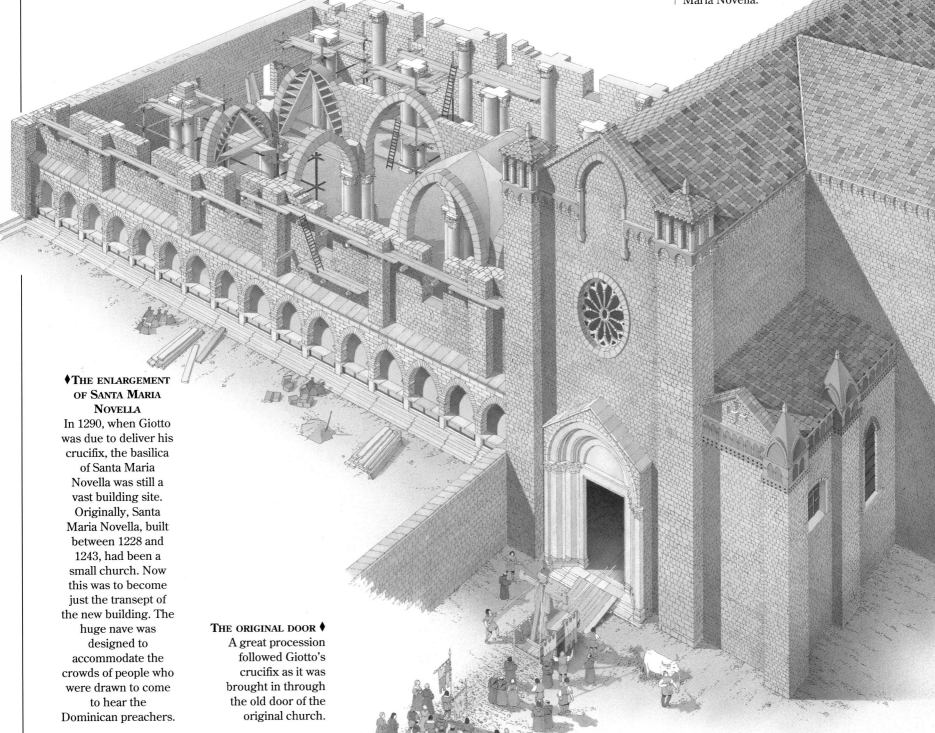

♦ THE ENLARGEMENT OF SANTA MARIA NOVELLA

In 1290, when Giotto was due to deliver his crucifix, the basilica of Santa Maria Novella was still a vast building site. Originally, Santa Maria Novella, built between 1228 and 1243, had been a small church. Now this was to become just the transept of the new building. The huge nave was designed to accommodate the crowds of people who were drawn to come to hear the Dominican preachers.

THE ORIGINAL DOOR ♦

A great procession followed Giotto's crucifix as it was brought in through the old door of the original church.

## ♦ CONVENTS

Workmen and merchants were attracted to Florence because of its rapid economic development and they settled in new suburbs outside the city walls of 1173-75. It was in these suburbs, close to the old city gates, that the mendicant orders established their houses, known as convents, in the 13th century. They preached poverty and charity, looked after the poor and sick and helped immigrants from the country learn one of the city's trades: textile manufacture, building work or crafts. The convents became the focal points of the city's growth.

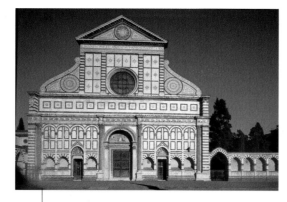

**♦ SANTA MARIA NOVELLA**
The church in Florence, as it appears today. Leon Battista Alberti's façade dates from the 15th century.

**6 ♦ GIOTTO'S LIFE STORY.** *An apprentice would normally leave his master's workshop and set up on his own between the ages of twenty-two and twenty-five. Giotto was not even twenty years old when he achieved independence. His first important commission was for a large crucifix for the Dominican church of Santa Maria Novella in Florence. The Dominicans had long held Cimabue in high esteem: in 1265 he had painted a great crucifix for the church of St Dominic in Arezzo. By 1285, the work to enlarge the church of Santa Maria Novella was so far advanced that the friars wanted to commission a crucifix to hang in the centre of the nave. They naturally turned to Cimabue, but the master was fully occupied and so he recommended his pupil Giotto.* ≫→

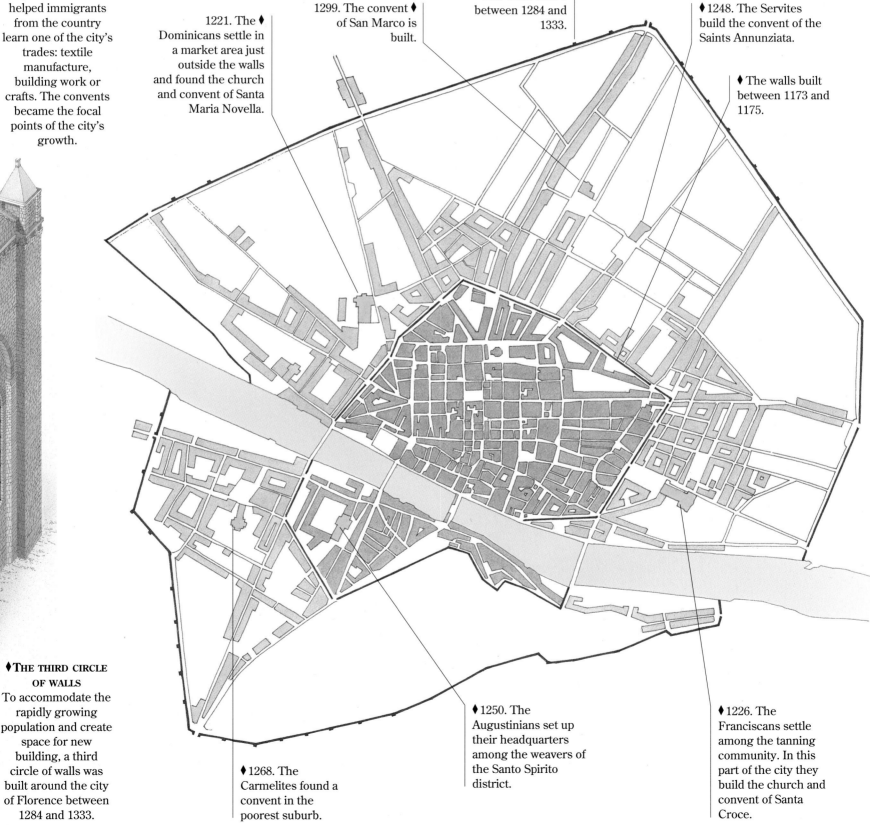

1221. The ♦ Dominicans settle in a market area just outside the walls and found the church and convent of Santa Maria Novella.

1299. The convent of San Marco is built.

The walls built ♦ between 1284 and 1333.

♦ 1248. The Servites build the convent of the Saints Annunziata.

♦ The walls built between 1173 and 1175.

♦ 1250. The Augustinians set up their headquarters among the weavers of the Santo Spirito district.

♦ 1226. The Franciscans settle among the tanning community. In this part of the city they build the church and convent of Santa Croce.

♦ 1268. The Carmelites found a convent in the poorest suburb.

## ♦ THE THIRD CIRCLE OF WALLS

To accommodate the rapidly growing population and create space for new building, a third circle of walls was built around the city of Florence between 1284 and 1333.

# CRUCIFIXES

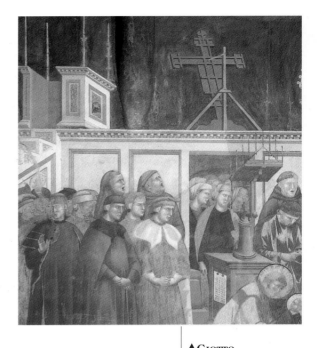
♦ **CIMABUE**
*Crucifix*, Florence,
c.1280 (Museo
dell'Opera di Santa
Croce).

♦ **COMPARISON**
Comparing an early
crucifix by Cimabue
(1265), below left,
with one done by
Giotto for the church
of Santa Maria
Novella, below right,
reveals how styles
developed. Cimabue's
crucifix is still
strongly influenced
by Byzantine
tradition. In his later
Santa Croce *Crucifix*
(above), now badly
damaged, Cimabue,
too, proved himself
an innovator. Giotto's
*Crucifix*, compared
with that of his
teacher, shows Christ
in a much more
natural pose.

Images of Christ on the cross date back a long way.
By the 4th century AD, the subject was common
throughout Christendom. It was carved in stone,
forged in metal, and shown in mosaics and fresco
paintings on church walls. Painted crucifixes came
later. Of impressive dimensions, they were hung
beneath the chancel arch or mounted on the screen
that separated the sanctuary, where the clergy
worshipped, from the nave, to which all had access.
Originally, such crucifixes were complex, both in form
and in the figures and symbols shown on them. The
Virgin Mary and St John, the mourning womenfolk,
and episodes from the life of Jesus were depicted on
either side of the central figure of Christ. The
Ascension of Christ and the Virgin with Angels were
shown in the space at the top. At the ends of the
horizontal bar of the cross were figures of Prophets
and scenes from the Passion. By the early 13th
century the central part of the cross was smaller and
decorated only with geometrical and flower motifs,
while half-length figures of the Virgin and St John
occupied the square panels at either end of the cross
bar. Subsequent changes were mainly stylistic.

♦ **GIOTTO**
*Institution of the crib
at Greccio* (detail),
from the Upper
Church of
St Francis, Assisi,
1290-95. The painting
provides evidence of
how crucifixes were
displayed in
churches.

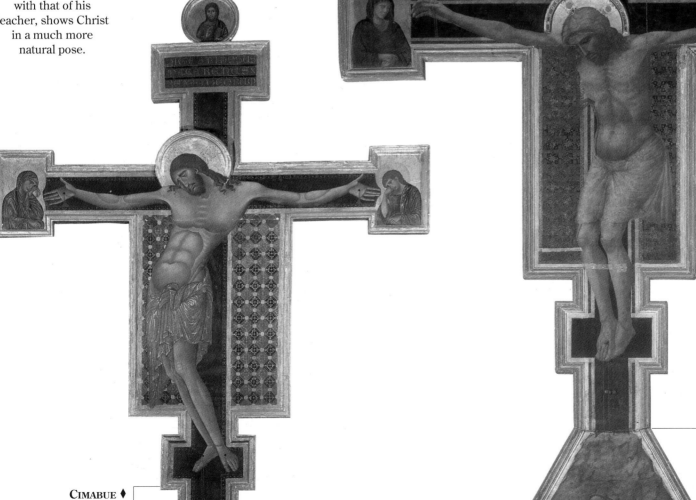

**CIMABUE** ♦
*Crucifix* at San
Domenico, Arezzo,
1265, 341 x 264 cm
(11 ft 2 in x 8 ft 7 in).

♦ **GIOTTO**
*Crucifix*, tempera on
wood, at Santa Maria
Novella, Florence,
1290, 578 x 406 cm
(18 ft 10 in x
13 ft 3 in).

# CIMABUE

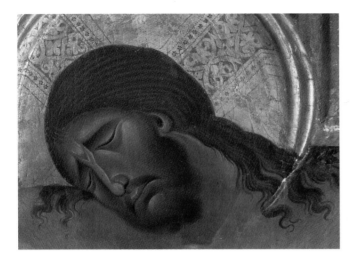

### ♦ THE HEAD
Christ's head is inclined to his right, and sinks into his collar bone. The hair falling onto his shoulders is neatly arranged. The knitted brows and tightly closed lips give his face an expression which communicates great suffering.

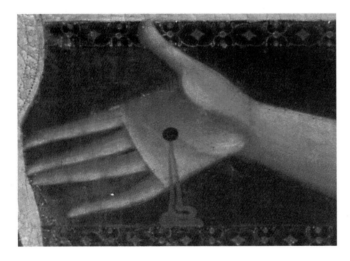

### ♦ THE HANDS
Cimabue represents the hands of Jesus in a stylized way, palms stretched out flat and the thumbs pointing upwards. The blood flowing from the wounds stops at the limit of the frame.

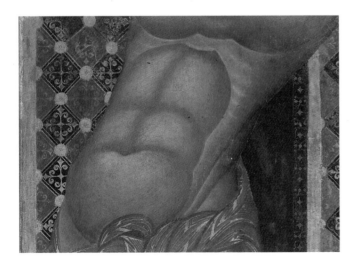

### ♦ THE TORSO
The pelvis is far over to the left, giving a curve to the whole figure. Little anatomical detail is shown. The stomach muscles are reduced to three horizontal bands. The style is abstract and symbolic.

# GIOTTO

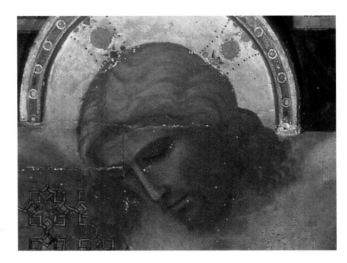

### ♦ THE HEAD
The head of Jesus falls forward. The hair, too, hangs downwards and in front of his right armpit. The facial features are relaxed. Giotto has shown the lips parted, a realistic detail of what happens at death.

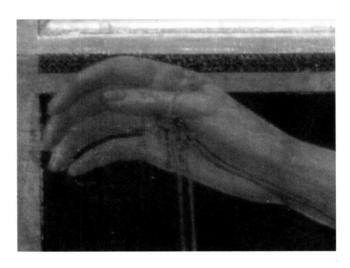

### ♦ THE HANDS
The hands are drawn in perspective. The thumbs are turned downwards and the fingers are slightly bent – realistic signs of a body relaxed in death. The blood from Christ's wounds also looks realistic.

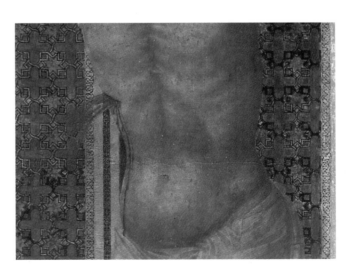

### ♦ THE TORSO
The body hangs with the pelvis only slightly to the right. The almost straight torso is shown with accurate anatomical detail. The jet of blood from the wound in Christ's side runs down onto his knee.

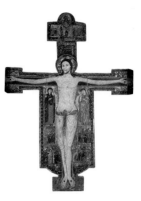

### ♦ GUGLIELMO DA SARZANA
*Crucifix with stories of the Passion*, 1138, Sarzana cathedral. This is the earliest surviving example of a painted crucifix. It bears the signature of the Ligurian painter Guglielmo da Sarzana and is dated 1138. Crucifixes from the 12th century depict Christ in a rigidly vertical position and looking still alive.

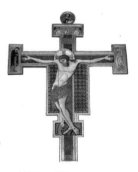

### ♦ THE MASTER OF ST FRANCIS
*Crucifix*, 1272 (Galleria Nazionale dell'Umbria, Perugia). Crucifixes from the 13th century represent Christ as a human figure already dead.
Painted crucifixes were unique to Italy. In some cases, the figures were painted directly onto a wooden panel. In others they were painted onto sheets of parchment or leather, and these were then applied to a cross-shaped wooden support.
The increasing concern that art should look true to life led to the decline of painted crucifixes in the 14th century, and to their replacement by works of sculpture.

# MEDIEVAL TRAVEL

We tend to think of travel as a relatively modern activity, related to the rapid development of transport systems in the 20th century. But people also travelled a great deal in medieval times, in spite of the many hardships involved. Of course, most people travelled on foot. Only noblemen and high-ranking churchmen were able to afford horses or covered wagons. It was common to travel in convoy: there was safety in numbers when it came to coping with natural dangers, highwaymen and pirates. People had two main reasons for undertaking a journey. Merchants travelled to buy and sell their wares. Pilgrims journeyed to visit holy places. Although travel was a common experience, this was not generally reflected by artists painting places. Giotto was the first to show much interest in portraying real landscapes, and the Sienese painters developed this. Landscapes did not become a usual subject of art until around 1400.

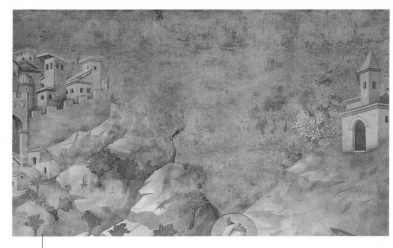

♦ **GIOTTO**
A detail from Giotto's *Francis giving his cloak to a poor knight*, Upper Church, Assisi, 1290-95. The hillside on the left is dotted with small trees. It rises in broad terraces to a fortified hill town, typical of the central Italian landscape. On the summit of the hillside to the right stands a religious building. In this scene, Giotto has represented some basic features, to give a convincing impression of the real natural environment.

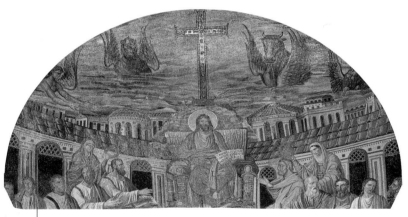

♦ **APSE MOSAIC**
Santa Pudenziana, Rome, 402-417. This mosaic does not give an impression of a real landscape and there is no overall sense of proportion. However, some details are represented in a realistic way: for example, the architectural features behind the enthroned Christ, the more distant buildings, and the reddish glow of the sunset.

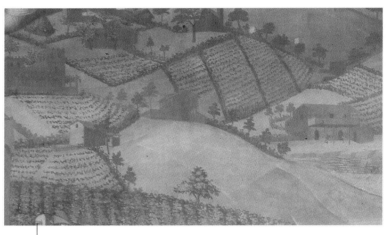

♦ **AMBROGIO LORENZETTI**
A detail from his fresco of *The effects of Good Government in town and country*, 1338-40 (Palazzo Pubblico, Siena). This shows a cultivated landscape typical of the Sienese countryside.

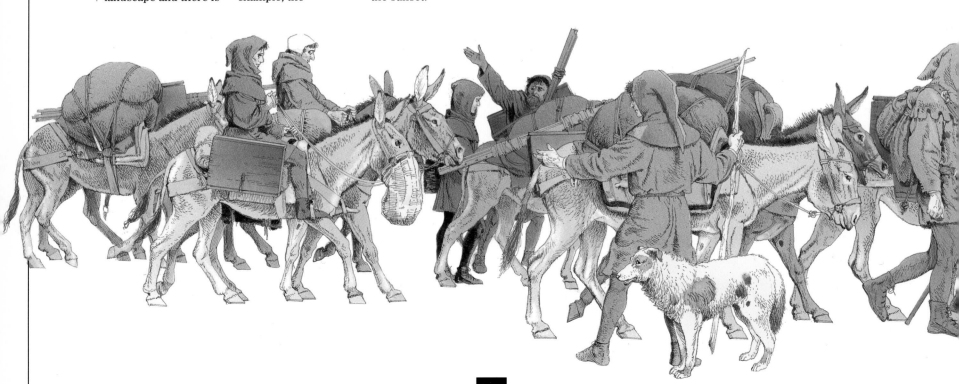

**Noli me tangere ♦ [Touch me not]**
A detail from Giotto's painting of Mary Magdalene's encounter with the risen Christ, 1302-06 (Scrovegni Chapel, Padua). Giotto did not attempt to show a life-like reproduction of the garden in which the meeting was said to take place, but he did depict some of the plants in the garden realistically. Parsley, celery and fennel are recognizable.

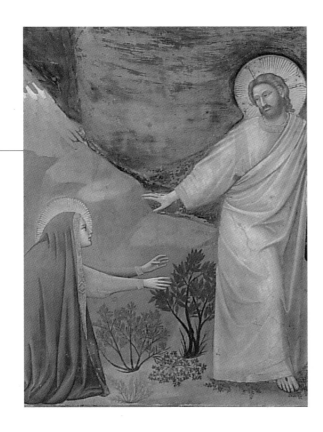

**7 ♦ GIOTTO'S LIFE STORY.** *In 1287 Giotto married a woman named Ciuta, which was short for Ricevuta. They had eight children. Some of them were to follow in their father's footsteps, although none was his equal as a painter. In Giotto's time, a son who took up the same occupation as his father was exempt from paying the admission fee to the guild of that occupation. This explains why a particular trade tended to run in the family. Though Giotto soon became a wealthy man, he did not forget the countryside of Mugello, where he had been born, and he bought large estates in the area. However, his success, and the resulting commissions from important patrons, led to his making frequent journeys up and down Italy. In central Italy, he undertook work in Assisi and Rome; in the south, in Naples; in the north, in Milan, Rimini, Ravenna and Padua.* ≫→

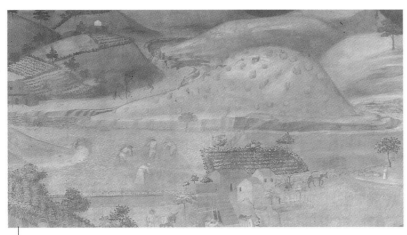

**AMBROGIO ♦ LORENZETTI**
*View of a town*, c.1340 (Pinacoteca, Nazionale, Siena). Landscape painting was pioneered by the Sienese, notably Lorenzetti. This detail from one of his paintings shows a typical walled medieval town with its look-out tower by the sea.

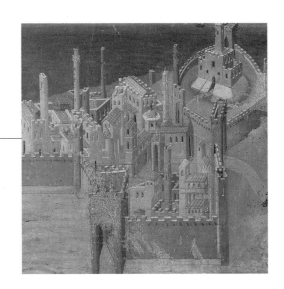

**♦ AMBROGIO LORENZETTI**
Another detail from *The effects of Good Government in town and country*. This was the first real attempt by an artist to paint the landscape for its own sake. It shows a hilly area and a cultivated plain.

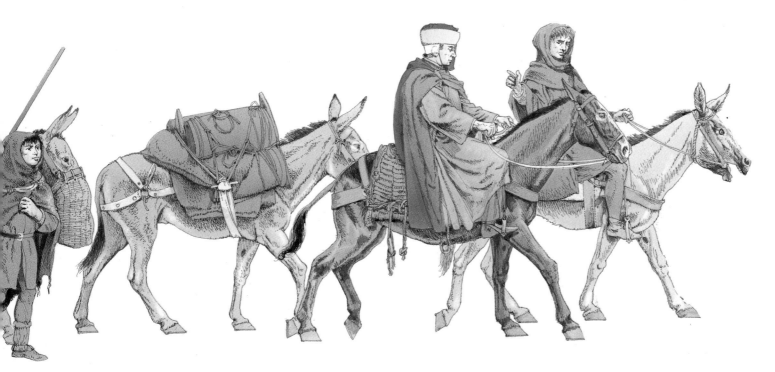

**♦ THE MASTER ON HIS TRAVELS**
A medieval master like Giotto, with his own workshop, had many assistants and apprentices working under him. His reputation for skilled craftsmanship was known far beyond his native area. Therefore, he would receive commissions from many parts of the country. He would travel to carry out important commissions, and the whole workshop staff would accompany him.

# THE CHURCHES AT ASSISI

In the 13th century, a small town in central Italy became a major centre of Christianity. Assisi's claim to fame was that St Francis (1181-1226) had been born and died there. A great two-storey basilica was erected at Assisi in his honour. The cut-away drawing on this page shows how the Upper and Lower Churches of St Francis were built one above the other. The walls were decorated from floor to ceiling with extraordinary effect. And the fresco paintings telling the story of the saint were not the only colourful features: the ceilings, ribbed vaulting and bases of the pilasters were also painted with brightly coloured geometric designs – all to an overall plan carefully thought out by the Franciscan friars. The work done here by German and French masters, Cimabue and Giotto, Simone Martini and artists from Rome amounted to a renewal of the art of painting.

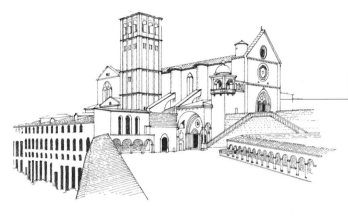

**♦ ONE CHURCH ABOVE ANOTHER**
The complex consists of a crypt and two basilicas, one built above the other. The closed-in atmosphere of the more humble Lower Church lends itself to meditation. The loftier Upper Church is more designed for preaching.

**MURAL PAINTING ♦**
The upper sections of wall were painted first. The sections reserved for the work of Giotto are shown in white.

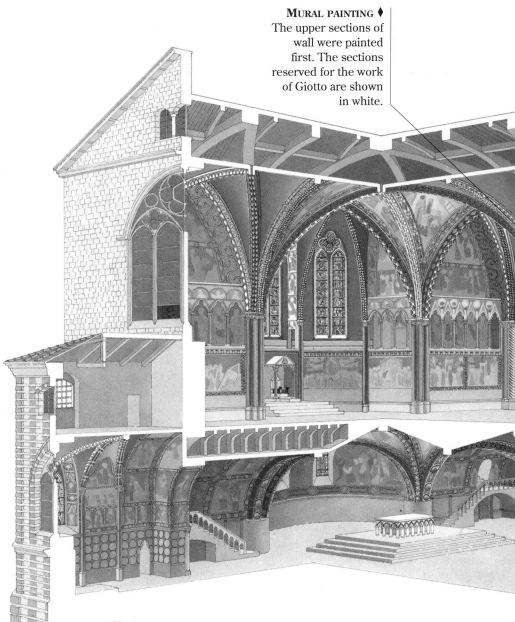

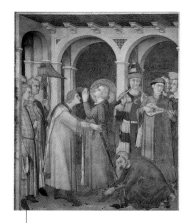

**♦THE INVESTITURE OF ST MARTIN**
A fresco by Simone Martini, in the Lower Church of St Francis, Assisi, c.1317.

**♦ STAINED GLASS**
For the first stained-glass windows, the Franciscans called on masters from France and Germany, because there were no artists skilled in this field in Italy. However, for the later windows, they were able to employ Italian craftsmen. Left: stained glass with *Stories of the life of St Francis*, Upper Church, Assisi.

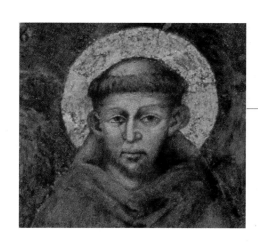

**♦ST FRANCIS**
A detail of Cimabue's portrait of the saint in the Lower Church of St Francis, Assisi, 1278-80.

**♦THE CRYPT**
The magnificent basilica was built partly to house the tomb of St Francis. His remains were placed in a crypt beneath the altar of the Lower Church. This crypt remained walled up until the 18th century, for fear of the tomb being desecrated by grave-robbers.

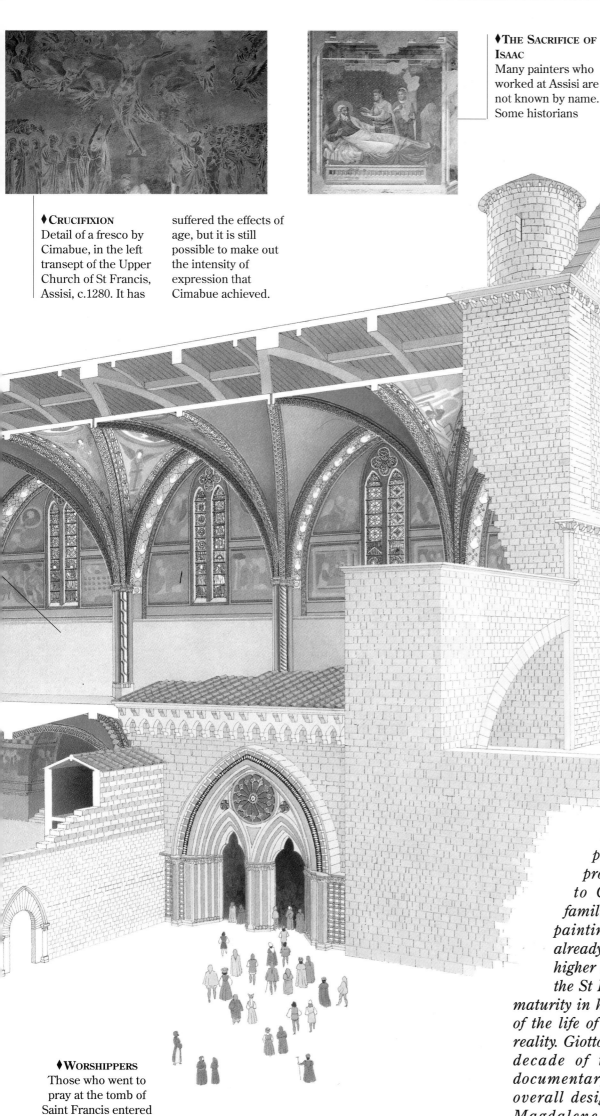

♦ **THE SACRIFICE OF ISAAC**
Many painters who worked at Assisi are not known by name. Some historians believe that this fresco in the Upper Church, by the Isaac Master, is in fact the work of Giotto.

♦ **THE BUILDING**
In 1228, the year in which Francis was canonized, Pope Gregory IX laid the foundation stone of the basilica, and in 1230 the body of the saint was buried there. The church was probably completed in 1280. During this period Italian architecture was freeing itself from Romanesque forms and adopting its own brand of the Gothic style. The façade is still Romanesque in character, while the pointed arches and buttresses are Gothic features.

♦ **CRUCIFIXION**
Detail of a fresco by Cimabue, in the left transept of the Upper Church of St Francis, Assisi, c.1280. It has suffered the effects of age, but it is still possible to make out the intensity of expression that Cimabue achieved.

♦ **ENTRANCE TO THE UPPER CHURCH**
This door was used by the great crowds of pilgrims who flocked to religious celebrations.

♦ **WORSHIPPERS**
Those who went to pray at the tomb of Saint Francis entered by the door of the Lower Church.

**8 ♦ GIOTTO'S LIFE STORY.** *Some time around 1290, Giotto came to Assisi to paint the life story of St Francis. He had probably been there before, while apprenticed to Cimabue, and had an opportunity to familiarize himself with the most recent trends in painting. Some scholars believe that Giotto had already painted some of the biblical scenes on the higher sections of wall, before he came to work on the St Francis cycle. But the artist reached his full maturity in his frescos of St Francis, telling the episodes of the life of the saint with a new concern for earthly reality. Giotto was to return to Assisi again in the second decade of the 14th century. Despite a lack of documentary evidence, many critics agree that the overall design for the chapel dedicated to St Mary Magdalene in the Lower Church is the work of Giotto himself, though executed by a large team of assistants.* ≫⁺

# THE FRANCISCANS

The Order of Friars Minor, or the Franciscans, was founded in 1209 by Francis of Assisi. Starting with only eleven brothers, it grew in numbers and importance throughout the 13th century. The papacy encouraged the order as a way of countering the heretical movements that were proliferating at that time. However, on-going disagreements between two factions of the Franciscans hindered the order's development to some extent. The Spirituals feared that ownership of property and magnificent religious buildings was not in keeping with the message of poverty preached by St Francis. The Conventuals, on the other hand, wanted the order to appear powerful in the eyes of ordinary believers. Their argument prevailed, and imposing churches began to be built in memory of the saint. Francis was an enormously popular figure, and the story of his life remained one of the favourite subjects of Italian painters until the 14th century.

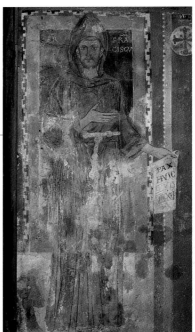

**ST FRANCIS ♦**
A fresco at Sacro Speco, Subiaco, 1228. This is one of the oldest images of St Francis, painted just two years after his death. It is an idealized representation rather than a realistic portrait. We know that Francis was in fact short and somewhat ugly, and had a defective eye.

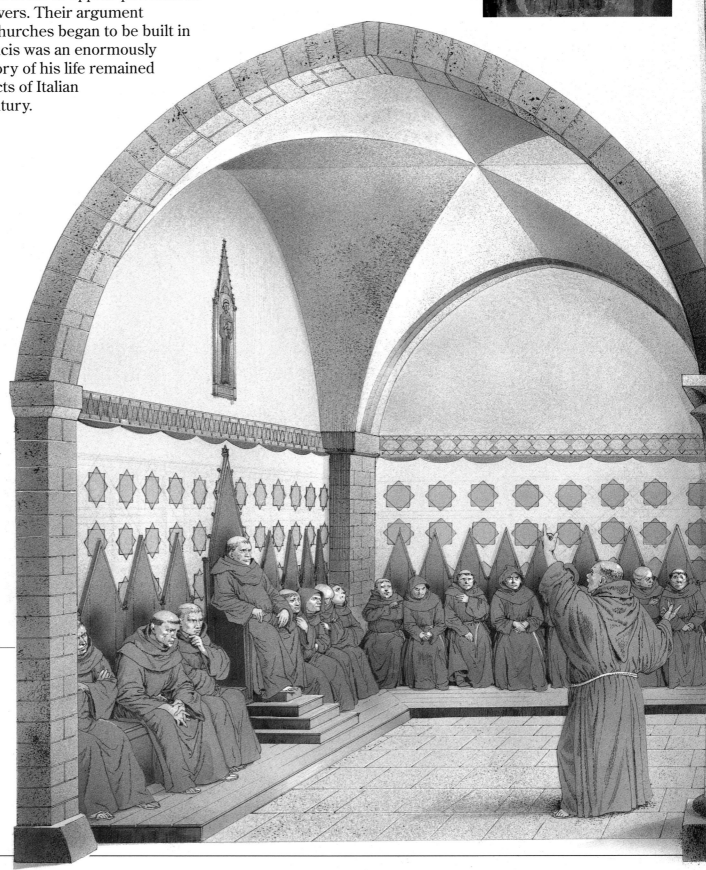

**MEETING OF THE ♦ FRANCISCAN CHAPTER**
A Franciscan pope, Nicholas IV, was elected in 1288, and this gave fresh impetus to the decoration of the basilica of St Francis in Assisi. After a great deal of discussion, the general assembly, or chapter, of Franciscan friars commissioned Giotto to paint the life story of St Francis. They insisted that the master take his subject matter from the official biography which had been written by St Bonaventure. This was now the only biography of the saint that the Franciscan order recognized as authentic. All earlier accounts, written by Francis's first followers, had been banned.

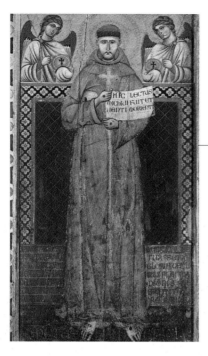

♦ ST FRANCIS
BETWEEN TWO ANGELS
Tempera on wood, by
the St Francis Master,
Santa Maria degli
Angeli, Assisi, second
half of the 13th
century. This work
was painted on the
wooden boards that
St Francis had used
for a bed. Depicted
again with the fixed
gaze of the ascetic,
the saint shows the
stigmata: the wounds
he is said to have
received, like Christ,
in hands, feet and
side.

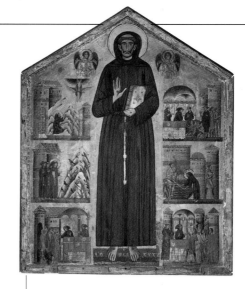

♦ ST FRANCIS,
WITH EPISODES
FROM HIS LIFE
An altar-piece by
Bonaventura
Berlinghieri, for
the church of
San Francesco at
Pescia, 1235. This
first representation of
the main events in
Francis's life portrays
him as an eastern
monk.

♦ ST FRANCIS
Born at Assisi in
1181, Francis was
half Italian and half
French in origin. His
mother, a native of
Provence, had him
baptized Giovanni.
However, on his
return from a
business trip to
France, his father,
Pietro Bernardone of
Lucca, insisted that
he be called
Francesco, the
Frenchman.

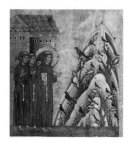

♦ ST FRANCIS
PREACHING TO THE
BIRDS
Bonaventura
Berlinghieri (detail).

After an ill-spent
youth, Francis
renounced his
inheritance and took
a vow of poverty,
devoting his life to
preaching simplicity,
humility and
brotherly love. He
founded a mendicant
order, approved by
Pope Innocent III as
the Friars Minor. On
his return from an
intended journey to
the Holy Land,
Francis contracted an
illness that left him
blind. In 1224, he
withdrew to the
mountain retreat of
La Verna in the
Casentino, where he
received the stigmata,
the marks of the
wounds sustained by
Christ. Francis died at
Assisi in 1226.

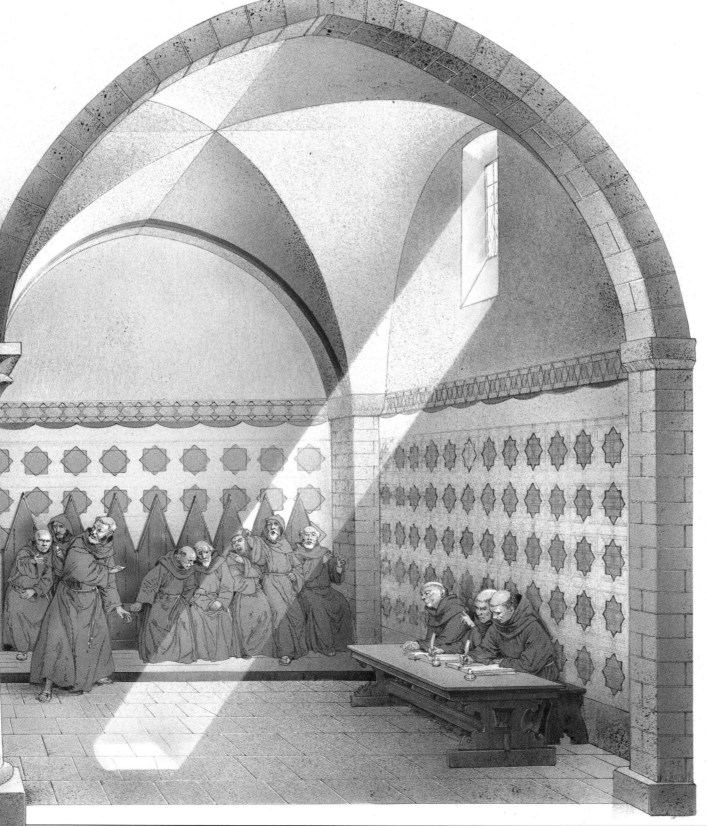

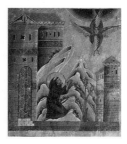

♦ ST FRANCIS
RECEIVING THE
STIGMATA
Bonaventura
Berlinghieri (detail).

# REAL LIFE

Largely due to the pioneering work of sculptors, 13th-century artists began to show the human figure, gestures and expressions in a new, realistic, rounded way. Giotto was one of the first artists to give the people in his paintings individual facial features and expressions. This realism was very different from the conventions of Byzantine painting, in which the human head was rigidly geometrical, presented full face or in profile, with wide-open, staring eyes and fixed, undifferentiated features betraying neither age nor feeling. By representing a wide range of gestures and expressions, the new generation of artists were able to humanize their characters and communicate feeling. The old conventions regarding clothing were also swept away. The new style of art no longer showed people dressed in Roman togas and mantles. It pictured them in their own everyday medieval clothing.

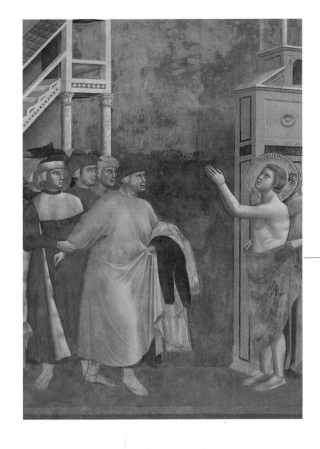

♦ **FRANCIS RENOUNCING HIS EARTHLY POSSESSIONS**
A detail from Giotto's work, Upper Church of St Francis, Assisi, 1290-95. The anger that is felt by Francis's father at his son's rejection of the family wealth shows in the intense, almost livid expression of his face and in the way he grasps his robe. If it had not been for the friend who is shown restraining him, he would have flown at his son. The father's anger is accentuated by the contrast with Francis's calm demeanour.

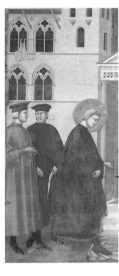

♦ **MEDIEVAL FASHION**
A detail from Giotto's work entitled *Homage of a simple man*, Upper Church of St Francis, Assisi, 1290-95. Giotto has shown the characters in contemporary dress, exemplifying men's fashion trends at the end of the 13th century. Francis is wearing a white cap, with his hair in neat rolls emerging at the back and sides.

♦ **REAL LIFE**
Giotto included elements of everyday life in his paintings, thanks to his keen observation of ordinary folk, the kind of people he might meet at the market.

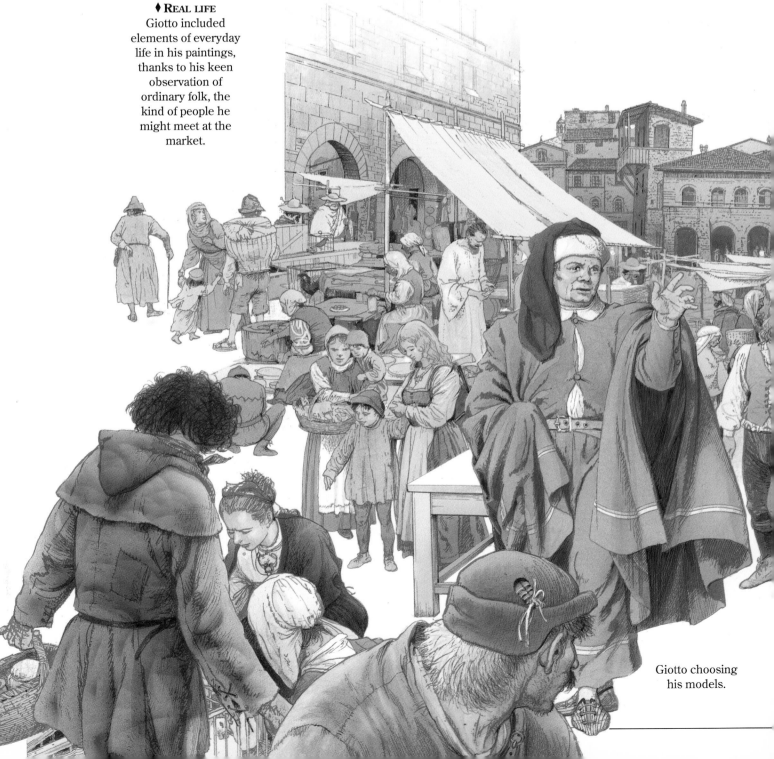

Giotto choosing his models.

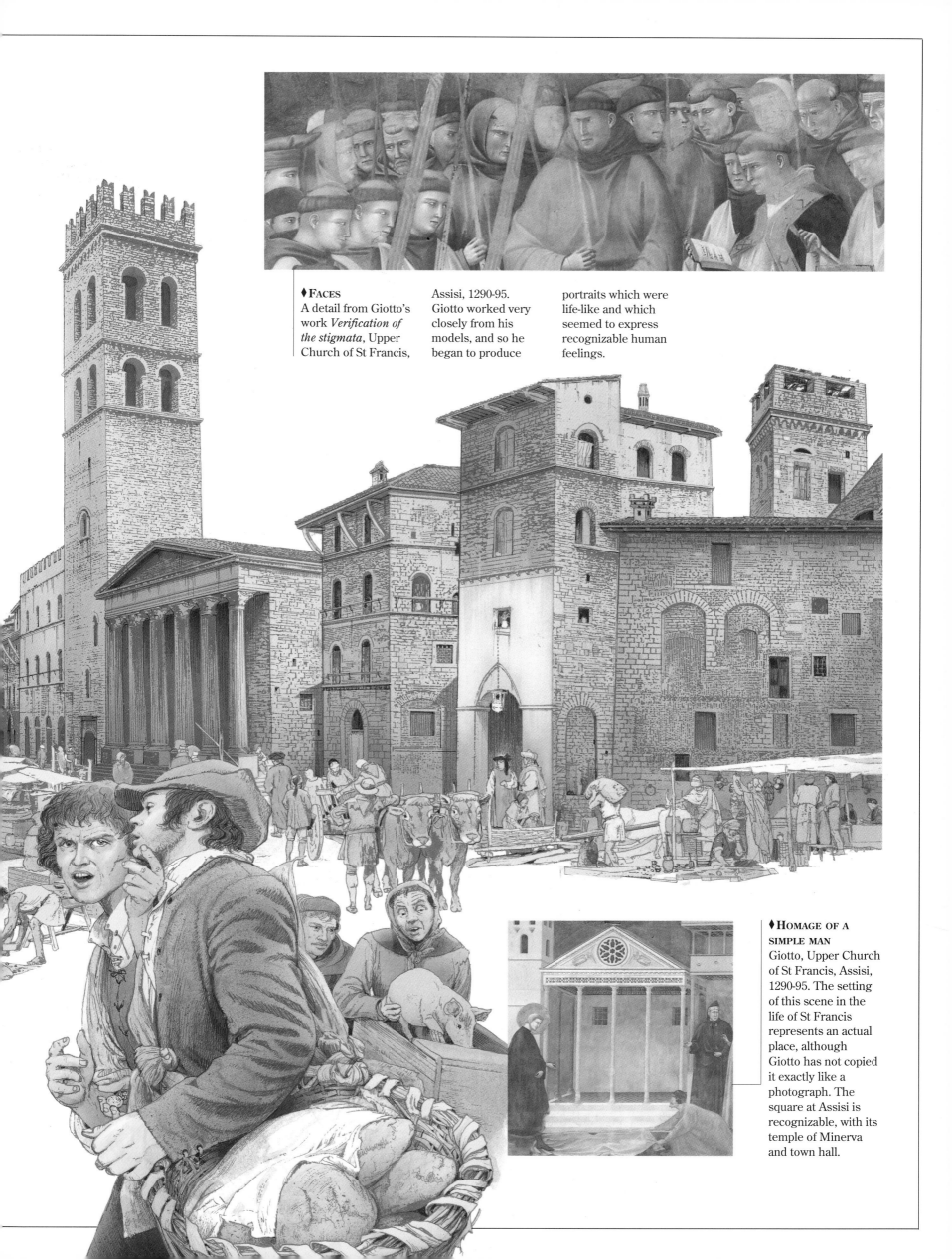

♦ FACES
A detail from Giotto's work *Verification of the stigmata*, Upper Church of St Francis, Assisi, 1290-95. Giotto worked very closely from his models, and so he began to produce portraits which were life-like and which seemed to express recognizable human feelings.

♦ HOMAGE OF A SIMPLE MAN
Giotto, Upper Church of St Francis, Assisi, 1290-95. The setting of this scene in the life of St Francis represents an actual place, although Giotto has not copied it exactly like a photograph. The square at Assisi is recognizable, with its temple of Minerva and town hall.

# FRESCO PAINTING

The fresco technique of wall or ceiling painting dates from classical times. Ancient Greek murals were probably painted in this way, and the ancient Roman ones of Pompeii most certainly were. The technique was little used in early Christian and medieval times, but it was revived in late 13th- and early 14th-century Italy. It consisted of applying paints (pigments mixed with water) to a still-wet layer of plaster (the *intonaco*), so that the colours would soak in and dry together with the support. Fresco painting was technically difficult: as it was done on wet plaster, the artist had to work quickly, finishing the day's portion of wall before the plaster dried. He also had to remember that the paint would change colour as it dried out. Correcting mistakes was difficult, for, once the paint had soaked into the plaster and dried, the artist could not begin again but only touch up his work by painting over it. Fresco paintings were done especially in Italy, and are also known in China and India. They survive well in dry climates, but not in places where damp gets into walls.

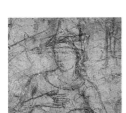

♦ **SINOPIA OF THE TRIUMPH OF DEATH**
A detail of a drawing by an unknown artist (Camposanta, Pisa).

♦ **SINOPIA**
A preliminary drawing of the fresco, called the sinopia, was made on the first, rough layer of plaster. Sinopia is a reddish-brown pigment. New techniques for removing frescos from walls have enabled us to recover some of these fascinating preliminary designs.

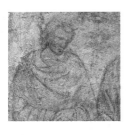

♦ **SINOPIA OF THE LAST JUDGEMENT**
A detail (Camposanta, Pisa).

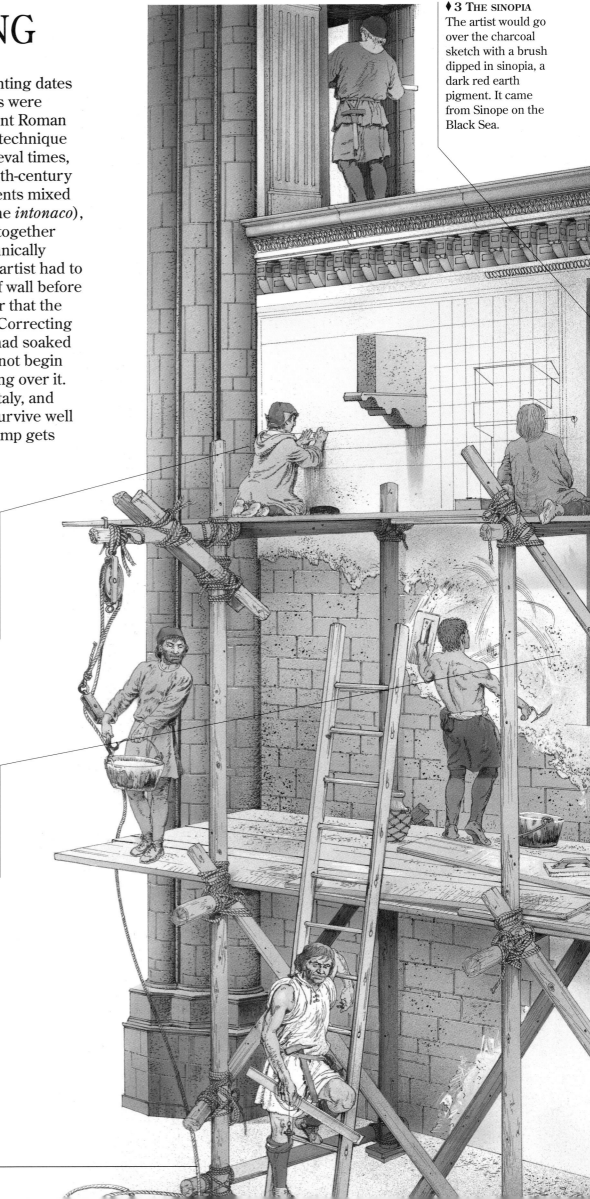

♦ **3 THE SINOPIA**
The artist would go over the charcoal sketch with a brush dipped in sinopia, a dark red earth pigment. It came from Sinope on the Black Sea.

**2 MARKING OUT** ♦
A line impregnated with chalk dust was used to mark out a grid on the rough plaster. This would guide the artist as he made a preliminary charcoal drawing.

**1 THE ARRICCIO** ♦
A plasterer would render the wall with a preliminary layer of rough plaster made from lime and sand. This layer was known as the *arriccio*.

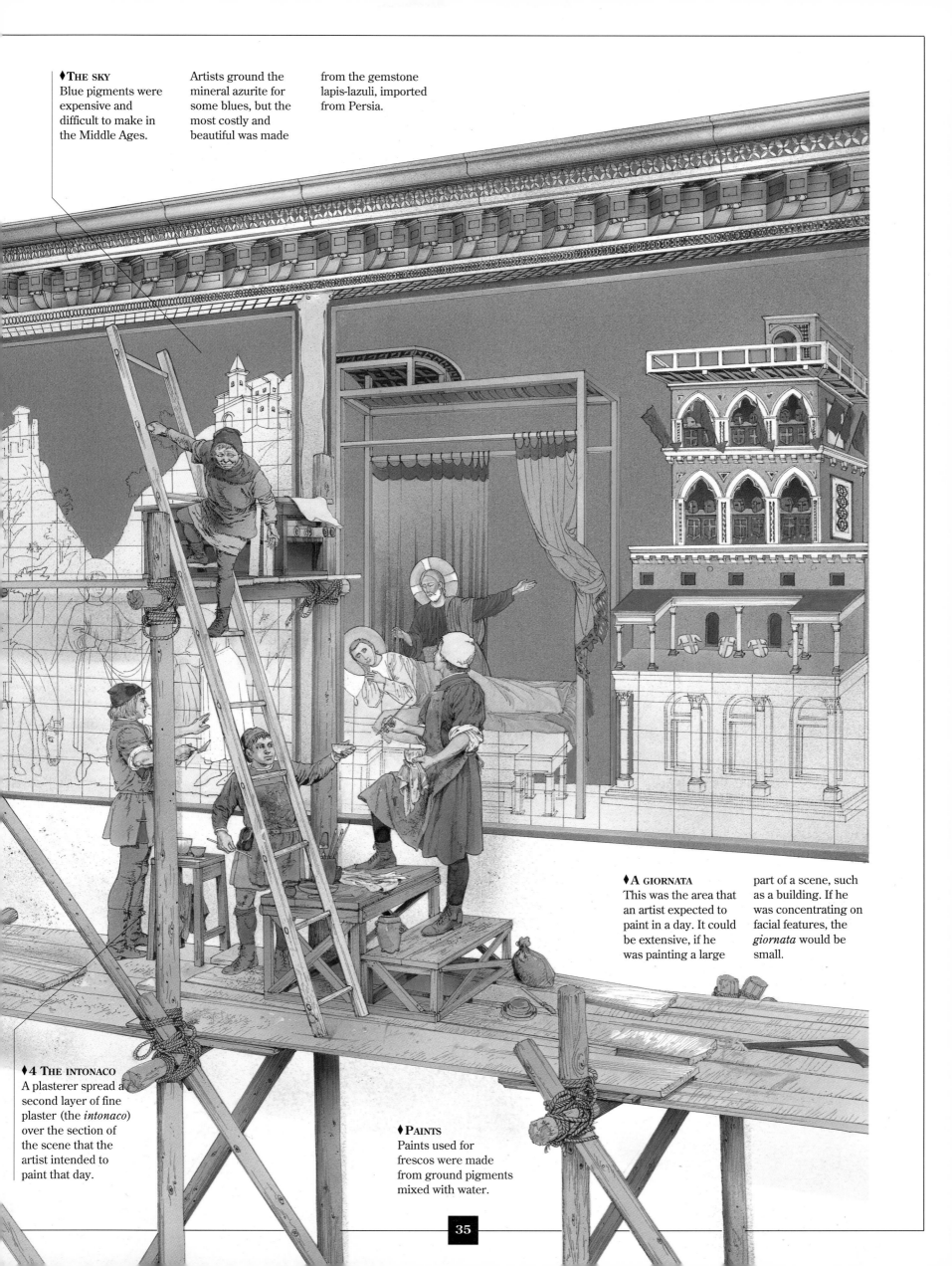

♦THE SKY
Blue pigments were expensive and difficult to make in the Middle Ages. Artists ground the mineral azurite for some blues, but the most costly and beautiful was made from the gemstone lapis-lazuli, imported from Persia.

♦A GIORNATA
This was the area that an artist expected to paint in a day. It could be extensive, if he was painting a large part of a scene, such as a building. If he was concentrating on facial features, the *giornata* would be small.

♦4 THE INTONACO
A plasterer spread a second layer of fine plaster (the *intonaco*) over the section of the scene that the artist intended to paint that day.

♦PAINTS
Paints used for frescos were made from ground pigments mixed with water.

# THE STORY OF ST FRANCIS

It was common for artists in the Middle Ages to paint a series of panels representing progressive scenes in a story. A famous cycle of frescos of this kind, depicting the life of St Francis, adorns the walls of the Upper Church of St Francis at Assisi. The cycle consists of twenty-eight panels around the lower part of the walls of the nave and entrance. They are arranged three to each window bay, with the exception of the first bay from the main door, which contains four panels. In the entrance, there is one scene on the wall on either side of the main door. Each panel representing an individual episode is framed by painted cornices and by painted barley-sugar columns left and right. The succession of events shown in the fresco cycle follows the story of the saint as set out in St Bonaventure's *Greater Life of St Francis*, written between 1260 and 1263. Giotto worked on the fresco cycle between 1290 and 1296. It is unlikely that he worked on his own, as the frescos vary in quality and some of the painting is not of the highest standard. It seems very likely that Giotto was responsible for the overall design and for the preparatory drawings, with a large team of helpers involved in the actual painting.

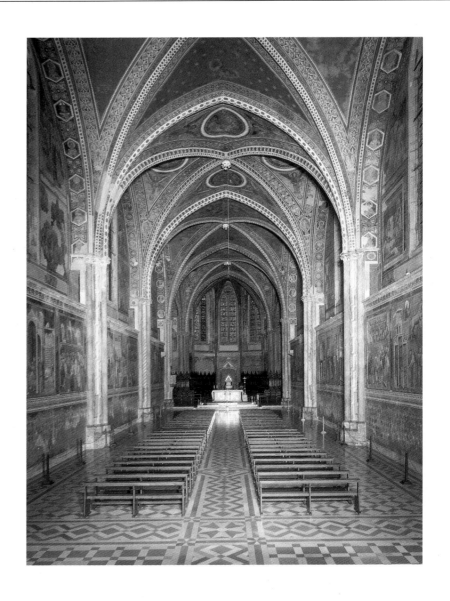

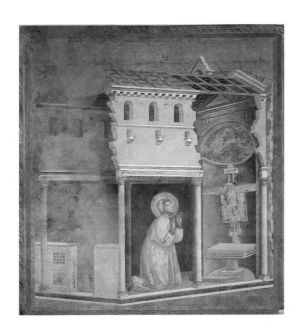

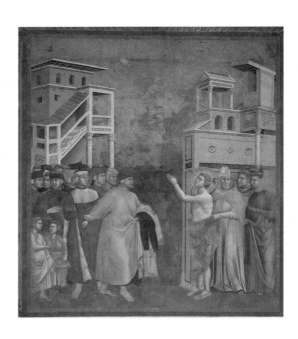

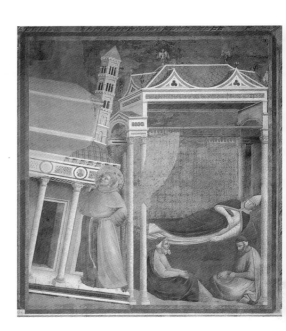

**4. THE MIRACLE OF THE CRUCIFIX**
One day Francis went out into the surrounding countryside, in order to meditate. Finding himself near the church of St Damian, which was badly dilapidated, he felt drawn to go in to pray. As he knelt before the image of Christ crucified, he heard the voice of God saying to him: "Go and repair my church, which, as you can see, is all in ruins."

**5. FRANCIS RENOUNCES HIS EARTHLY POSSESSIONS**
To follow his religious vocation, Francis decided to leave his family and the chance of a secure future. His father tried to win him back by forcing him, in the presence of the bishop, to give up all he had received from his family. Francis gave back his rich clothes, to show that he rejected his heritage. Moved by this, the bishop covered him with his own cloak.

**6. THE DREAM OF INNOCENT III**
When Francis went to Rome, to obtain confirmation of his rule and authorization to preach, Pope Innocent III had a dream which removed any doubt about Francis's future. He saw the basilica of St John Lateran about to topple. But it was prevented from crashing to the ground by a man of humble appearance, who came to support the building on his shoulder.

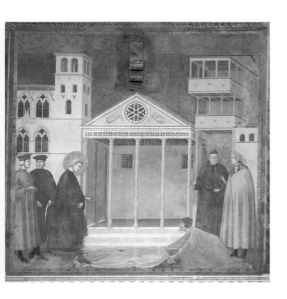

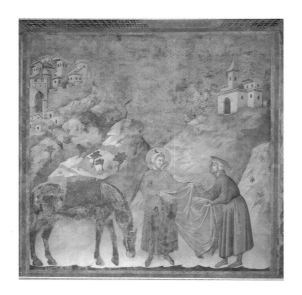

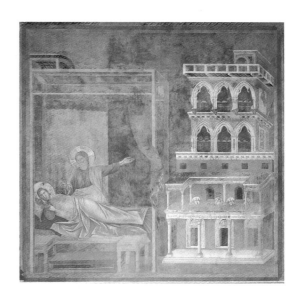

**1. THE HOMAGE OF A SIMPLE MAN**
An ordinary citizen of Assisi met Francis in the streets of the town and, inspired by God, spread out his cloak for Francis to walk on. The man claimed that Francis was worthy of all reverence, as he would soon do great things and would come to be honoured by all Christians. The scene is set in the main square of Assisi, with the temple of Minerva in the background.

**2. FRANCIS AND THE POOR KNIGHT**
One day Francis met a noble knight who had fallen on hard times. Feeling pity at the man's poverty, he took off his own cloak and gave it to him. Giotto set this episode in the vicinity of Assisi, which can be seen on the left. Francis's face expresses tenderness and compassion, while the knight's gaze is fixed on his benefactor.

**3. THE DREAM OF THE PALACE**
The following night, as Francis slept, God showed him in a dream a magnificent palace, full of armour bearing the sign of Christ's cross. The dream was to tell him that the compassion he had shown towards the poor knight would soon be rewarded by a great gift. In this fresco, Francis is depicted sleeping with his head resting on his right hand.

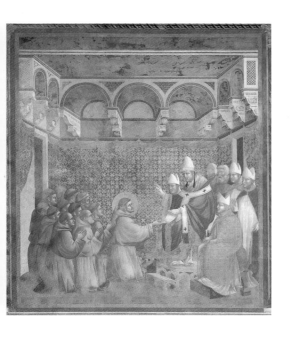

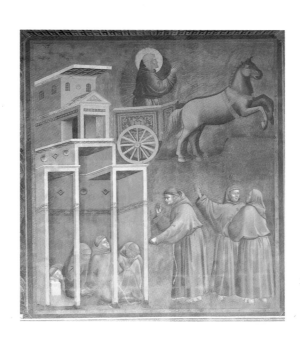

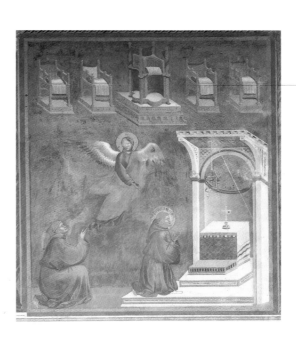

**7. CONFIRMATION OF THE RULE**
Pope Innocent III, now full of respect and veneration for Francis, approved his rule and authorized the young man to preach repentance. In this scene, Francis, shown with a beard for the first time, kneels before the Pope to receive the rule. The brothers kneeling behind him are depicted with the tonsure, the hair-style typical of Franciscan friars.

**8. THE VISION OF THE FLAMING CHARIOT**
One night Francis was praying with some of the brothers while others slept. Suddenly, a magnificent chariot of fire came and swept through the house in a blaze of glory. The brothers who saw it were amazed. The sleepers woke up terrified. But all knew that the Spirit of God had descended from heaven and was present among them.

**9. THE VISION OF THE THRONES**
On one occasion, a monk had entered an abandoned church with Francis to pray. In a moment of religious vision, he saw a number of thrones in heaven, one of which, more sumptuous than the others, was adorned with precious stones and bright with glory. As he wondered who the throne was for, a voice told him that it was reserved for the humble Francis.

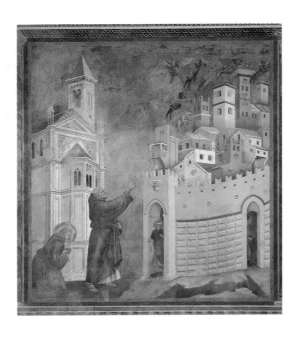

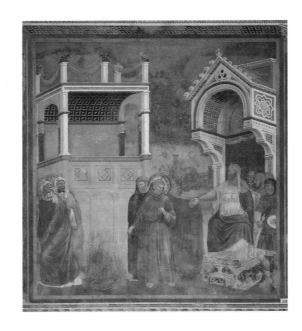

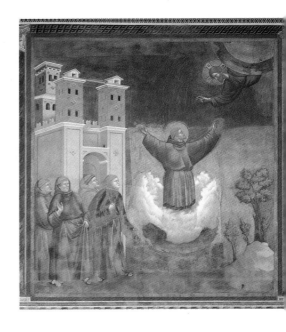

**10. THE EXPULSION OF THE DEMONS FROM AREZZO**
Francis came to Arezzo at a time of bitter civil
strife. From the outlying suburb where he was
staying, he saw exultant demons hovering over
the city, inciting the inhabitants to murder.
He asked Brother Sylvester to stand at the city gate
and order the demons to be gone. The friar did as
he was told, the demons fled, and peace was
immediately restored.

**11. TRIAL BY FIRE BEFORE THE SULTAN**
During the crusade of 1217-21, Francis went to the
Sultan of Egypt to try to convert him to
Christianity. To demonstrate the power of the
Christian faith, he challenged the Sultan's holy
men to undergo with him the ordeal of walking
through fire. They refused to take up this
challenge. They presented Francis with precious
gifts, which he scornfully rejected.

**12. THE ECSTASY OF ST FRANCIS**
At night Francis would seek out lonely places or
abandoned churches in which to pray. On one
occasion his brother friars saw him praying
fervently with his arms stretched out as on the
cross, raised off the ground and wrapped in a
luminous cloud. Giotto depicted him in this
posture, with Christ reaching down from the
heavenly realms in an act of blessing.

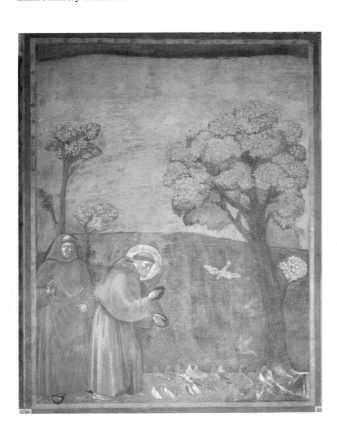

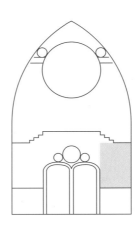

The position of the
fresco of *Francis
preaching to the birds*,
beside the main door
of the Upper Church
at Assisi.

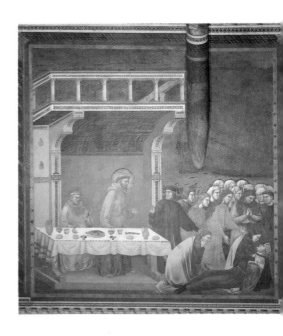

**15. FRANCIS PREACHES TO THE BIRDS**
Having received God's commission to go to
preach to all creation, Francis set off full of
enthusiasm and, on his way to Bovagna, near
Perugia, came to a place where a noisy flock of
birds of all kinds was gathered together. On
seeing him, the birds approached and fell silent.
He spoke to them as if to reasonable beings,
telling them always to praise their Creator.

**16. THE DEATH OF THE KNIGHT OF CELANO**
Once, when Francis was preaching at Celano, a
knight from the neighbourhood invited him for a
meal. Foreseeing that the knight would soon die,
Francis asked him to make his confession and to
set his household affairs in order. As the guests
were sitting down to table, the knight did suddenly
die. He had made his confession, and so he
entered heaven in a state of grace.

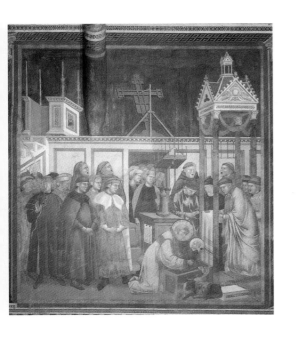

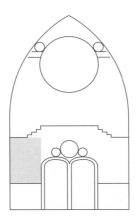

The position of the fresco of *The miracle of the spring*, beside the main door of the Upper Church at Assisi.

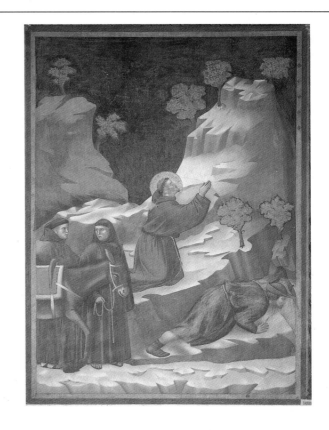

**13. THE INSTITUTION OF THE CRIB AT GRECCIO**
Three years before his death, in order to encourage a spirit of worship in ordinary people, Francis had a crib set up in a cave near Greccio, complete with a manger and a real ox and donkey. He thus started the tradition, which continues to this day, of preparing a crib at Christmas time in memory of Christ's birth in the stable at Bethlehem.

**14. THE MIRACLE OF THE SPRING**
One day Francis was unwell. He rode up to his mountain retreat of La Verna on a donkey lent him by a peasant, who followed on foot. Distressed and exhausted by the heat, the poor man pleaded for a drink. Francis got off the donkey and knelt to pray, whereupon water sprang from the bare rock. The spring was never found again.

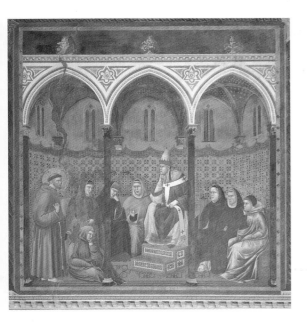

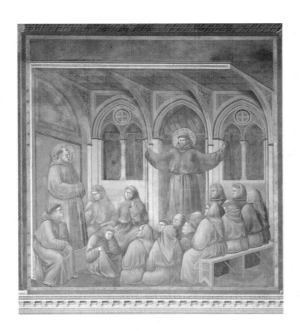

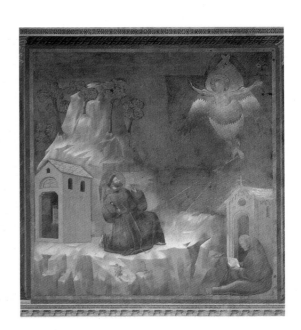

**17. FRANCIS PREACHES BEFORE HONORIUS III**
When Francis appeared before Pope Honorius III and his cardinals, his preaching was so sincere and effective that it was clear to them that his words were not merely the result of learned theological study but were inspired by God. Giotto's fresco captures the rapt attention of the Pope and cardinals, who appear to hang on Francis's every word.

**18. THE APPARITION AT ARLES**
One day, when St Anthony of Padua was preaching in the chapter house at Arles, taking as his subject the inscription on Christ's cross: "Jesus of Nazareth, King of the Jews", St Francis miraculously appeared to the brethren. Giotto has portrayed the saint as larger than the other figures, raised off the ground and with his arms extended in blessing.

**19. FRANCIS RECEIVES THE STIGMATA**
One day, when Francis had been praying and fasting at La Verna, Christ appeared to him in the form of a seraph and impressed on his hands, feet and side the marks of the nails and the lance which he himself had sustained on the cross. In this way, God answered the longing of Francis's heart: to be like Christ in his sufferings, before he died.

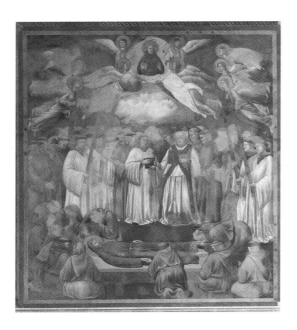

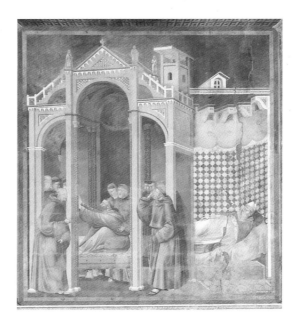

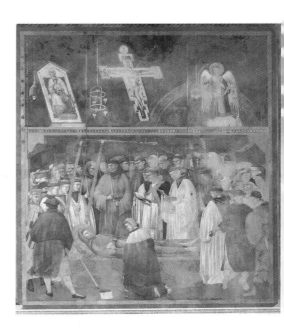

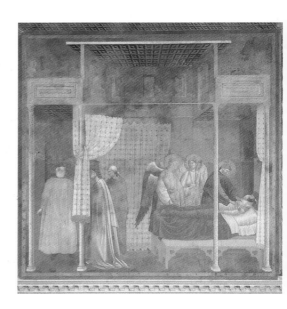

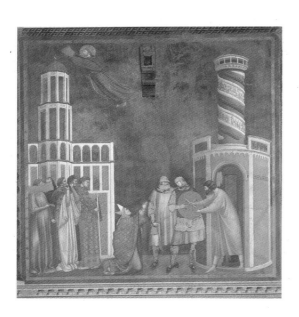

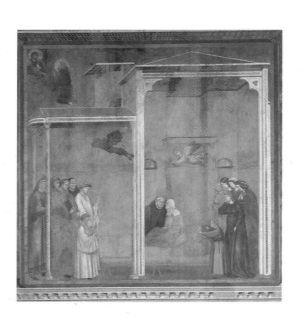

**20. THE DEATH OF ST FRANCIS**
When Francis died, one of the brethren saw his soul, which was now freed from his body, wing its way towards heaven surrounded by a white cloud. It looked like a bright shining star. Giotto's fresco captures the grief of the friars who are gathered around Francis's lifeless body, as they weep, pray, touch him, give way to despair or share their sorrow.

**21. THE APPARITION TO FRA AGOSTINO**
In a convent near Naples, at the very moment that Francis died, a brother called Agostino, who had been dumb for years and was near to death, cried out: "Wait for me, father, I want to go with you!" At the same time, in the oratory of St Michael on Mount Gargano, the bishop of Assisi had a vision of Francis saying: "I am leaving the world and going to heaven."

**22. VERIFICATION OF THE STIGMATA**
On hearing of Francis's death, people flocked to witness the marks of Christ's passion. Many citizens of Assisi were permitted to contemplate and even kiss the stigmata, among them a knight called Gerolamo. He was a doubter, like the apostle Thomas, and insisted on touching the stigmata. His doubts then removed, he became a faithful witness to the truth.

**26. FRANCIS HEALS THE MAN OF LÉRIDA**
In the town of Lérida, in Catalonia, Spain, a man named John had received a fatal wound in an ambush. Given up for lost by the doctors, and abandoned by his wife, who feared infection, he cried out repeatedly to St Francis. The saint appeared to him, removed his bandages, gently dressed his wounds with an ointment and effected a complete cure.

**27. THE CONFESSION OF THE WOMAN OF BENEVENTO**    At Monte Murano in the neighbourhood of Benevento, Francis brought a woman back from the dead, so that she could be freed of a sin she had failed to confess in her lifetime. Giotto depicted the devil being forced to flee and make way for an angel, a sign that the woman had been purified and could now die in a state of grace.

**28. THE LIBERATION OF PETER THE HERETIC**
A man accused of heresy and imprisoned by the Bishop of Tivoli called on the aid of St Francis. When the saint appeared, the man's shackles fell off and the prison doors burst open. The man's cries of amazement alerted the guard, who reported the matter to the bishop. Recognizing the evidence of divine intervention, the bishop knelt and worshipped God.

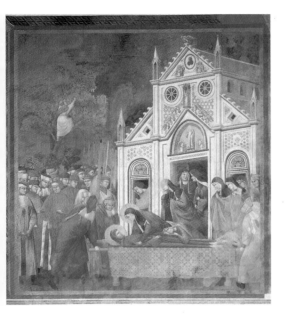

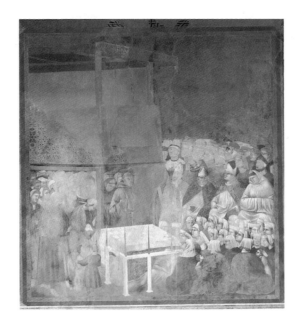

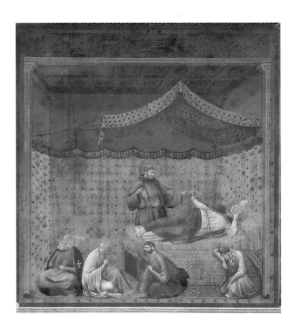

**23. THE LAMENT OF THE POOR CLARES**
The funeral procession stopped in front of the church of St Damian. The convent attached to the church was the home of St Clare and her sister nuns, to whom Francis had been a spiritual father. Clare and her companions embraced St Francis for the last time. The fresco shows the great crowd of mourners and St Clare bending over the body of St Francis.

**24. THE CANONIZATION OF ST FRANCIS**
On 16 July 1228, Pope Gregory IX came in person to Assisi to canonize Francis, officially declaring him a saint. The solemn ceremony was attended by the friars, a significant group of princes and barons, and a great crowd of ordinary people. Although this fresco has deteriorated, Giotto's skill in portraying realistic human features is still very evident.

**25. THE DREAM OF POPE GREGORY IX**
Before he canonized Francis, Pope Gregory had had some doubts about the mark of Christ's wound in his side. Then he had a dream in which Francis appeared to him to set his mind at rest. In this dream, Francis said: "Give me an empty flask." Gregory did as he was asked, and the bottle was miraculously filled with blood from the wound in Francis's side.

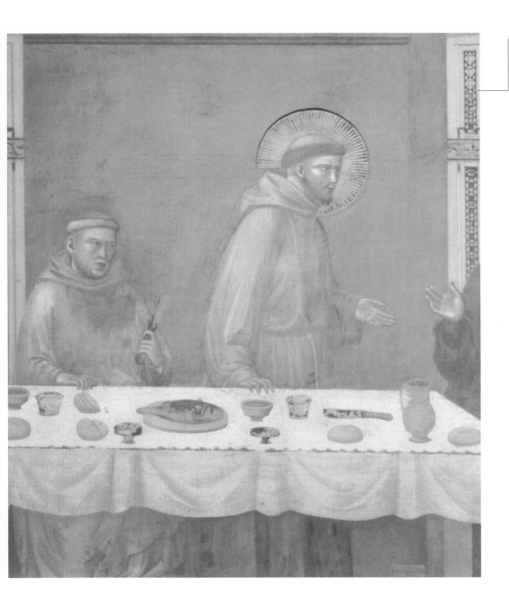

♦THE DEATH OF THE
KNIGHT OF CELANO
Detail, Upper Church
of St Francis, Assisi.

It is easy to see that, as well as being part of a series, each of the panels in the St Francis cycle pictures a single event in the life of the saint and is complete in itself. Francis appears in twenty-six of the twenty-eight panels (that is, all except numbers 21 and 24). He is shown in profile or full face, standing, kneeling or lying down, alive or dead, on earth or in heaven. He can be recognized by the halo, which indicates his holiness, and, apart from in the scenes of his early life, by his brown habit. Giotto followed the official biography of St Francis, written by St Bonaventure, very closely indeed. Because the Church was not entirely happy about the "holy poverty" preached by Francis, the biography – and therefore the fresco cycle – put more stress on Francis's miracle-working powers and on his close relationship with the popes.

# Jubilee year in Rome

In 1300, harking back to an ancient Hebrew festival called Jubilee, Pope Boniface VIII declared a holy year: three hundred and sixty-five days during which the Catholic Church would pardon sins. Exceptional indulgences were offered during this period to pilgrims who visited the four major churches of Rome: St Peter's, St John Lateran, Santa Maria Maggiore and St Paul's Outside the Walls. The city was crowded with visitors from all over Europe. Soon after, in 1309, Rome lost its predominant position in Christendom, when for almost seventy years the residence of the popes was transferred to Avignon, France. The jubilee year of 1300 was therefore one of the last occasions for which a medieval pope commissioned major works of art in Italy. Giotto was invited to work in Rome and he took advantage of this opportunity to study the work of the Roman artists more closely. Their particular strength was in the use of colour. Giotto's Roman works were carried out at different times and the majority of them have been lost. However, following a recent cleaning operation, a panel painting entitled the *Madonna della Minerva* is now thought to be by his hand.

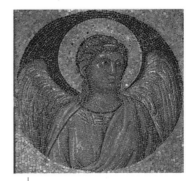

♦ **ANGEL**
(San Pietro Ispano, Boville Ernica, Frosinone). This mosaic angel is probably a fragment of the Navicella mosaic, although it is difficult to see what place it occupied in the picture as a whole. The angel may have supported the inscription at the bottom.

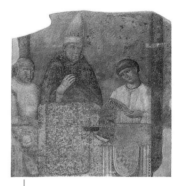

♦ **BONIFACE VIII PROCLAIMS THE JUBILEE**
(St John Lateran, Rome). This is the only remaining fragment of a fresco by Giotto and his assistants, which also included *The Baptism of Constantine* and *The Building of St John Lateran*.

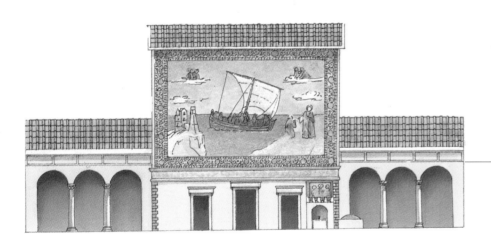

♦ **THE NAVICELLA**
The mosaic representing the boat of the disciples, tossed by the unexpected storm on Lake Galilee, was meant to attract the attention of pilgrims who had gathered in front of St Peter's.

**9 ♦ GIOTTO'S LIFE STORY.** *Some modern historians believe that, while living at Assisi and working on the fresco cycle of the Life of St Francis, Giotto made several trips to Rome. His purpose would have been to broaden his outlook by studying classical painting and the works of the Roman artist Pietro Cavallini, who was probably a strong influence on Giotto. It is, in any case, certain that Giotto returned to Rome in 1300 to paint a fresco in the loggia of St John Lateran, showing Pope Boniface VIII instituting the jubilee year. He was also in Rome in 1310, to execute the huge mosaic of the Navicella, or the Ship of the Church, in the portico of St Peter's. In around 1320, he painted the Stefaneschi altar-piece, or triptych, for the Roman Cardinal Stefaneschi. It is considered to be one of the great works of his mature career.* ➡

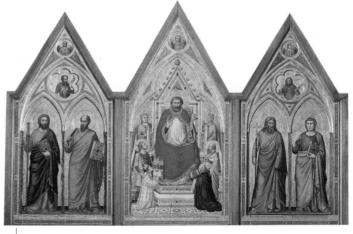

♦ **THE STEFANESCHI TRIPTYCH**
c.1320 (Pinacoteca Vaticana, Rome). Commissioned for the high altar of St Peter's, the triptych was painted on both sides. The panels displayed to the worshippers show Saints James and Paul; St Peter flanked by saints, angels and Cardinal Stefaneschi; and Saints Andrew and John the Evangelist.

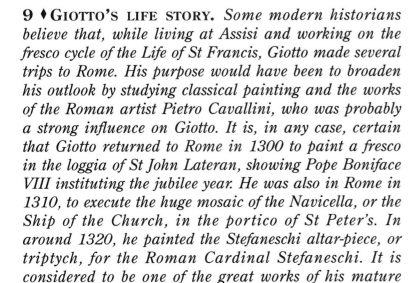

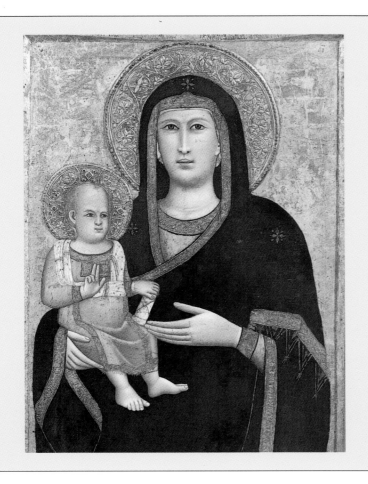

♦ **THE MADONNA DELLA MINERVA** (Private collection). Art historians often need to reassess an artist's career, in the light of new discoveries. As recently as 1993, a panel painting entitled the *Madonna della Minerva*, painted in Rome at the end of the 13th century, was attributed to Giotto. The work is thought to belong to the period when Boniface VIII was pope (1294-1303). It was painted after the fresco cycle at Assisi and before Giotto began work at the Arena Chapel in Padua.

The figures of the Madonna and Child were repainted as early as the 15th cen-

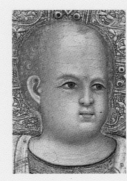

tury, and the golden background was restored in the 16th century. In the 17th century, the whole picture was painted over with oil paints. Cleaning has brought to light the original painting, in a surprisingly good state of preservation. According to ancient sources, the panel was painted for the altar of the Altieri chapel in Santa Maria sopra Minerva in Rome. Although it has the three-dimensionality which is characteristic of Giotto's work, it also adheres fairly closely to Byzantine conventions, which were still in fashion in late 13th-century Rome.

(*Below,* a detail of the right hand of the Child).

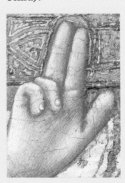

♦ **THE FIRST CHURCH**
Between 315 and 350, Constantine, the first Christian Roman emperor, had a basilica built over the tomb of the apostle Peter in Rome.

**ST PETER'S** ♦
The first church of St Peter is shown in red on this plan. The extent of St Peter's today is shown in yellow. The transformation of the church, which began in the 15th century, was completed in the 17th century.

♦ **THE BUILDING GIOTTO KNEW**
A view of St Peter's and the four-sided portico, as it was in Giotto's time.

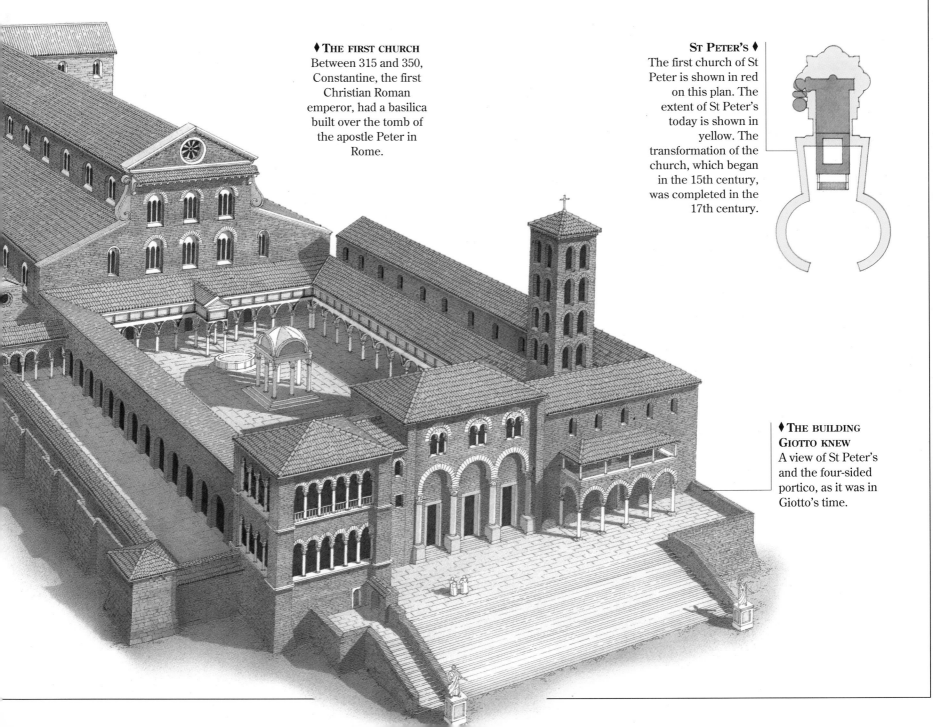

# ROMAN MOSAIC WORK

In the 13th century in Florence, the bishop, religious orders and rich banking and merchant families all took an interest in commissioning artists to produce work for them. In Rome it was different: commissions for works of art came almost exclusively from the pope and his court. The Romans were as yet untouched by the wind of change that was blowing through Florence. They were more traditional in their outlook and their attachment to the past was evident in their choice of decorative techniques: the Byzantine-style mosaic was still dominant there. In the second half of the 13th century, close links were formed between Florentine and Roman artists, and they influenced one another. Visits by Cimabue (known to have been in Rome in 1272) and Arnolfo di Cambio (1276) aroused new interest in the representation of the human figure, facial expressions and gestures. The most famous Roman masters were Pietro Cavallini, Jacopo Torriti and Filippo Rusuti. Contact with them and their work helped the Florentines to develop their use of colour. A major work of the period was a mosaic by Cavallini for the apse of Santa Maria in Trastevere.

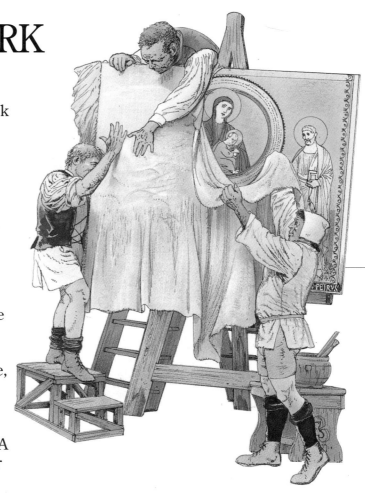

♦ **THE MEDIEVAL TECHNIQUE**
From the 13th century, mosaics were created as follows:
a) the *tesserae* were stuck provisionally to a wooden panel using a water-soluble glue.
b) a strong piece of canvas was glued over the mosaic, again using a water-soluble adhesive.
c) the mosaic was detached from its support and rolled up in the canvas.
d) the canvas was applied to the freshly-plastered wall and the *tesserae* pressed well into the plaster.
e) the plaster was left to dry.
f) the canvas was soaked in water, then removed.

♦ **PIETRO CAVALLINI**
Born in around 1250, Cavallini lived to be almost a hundred. He worked in the main churches in Rome and Naples, for important patrons such as King Charles of Naples and members of the papal court. The oldest surviving work bearing Cavallini's signature is a mosaic for Santa Maria in Trastevere, Rome. It depicts episodes from the Life of the Virgin. He then painted frescos for the church of Santa Cecilia in Trastevere, including a *Last Judgement* which was rediscovered in 1901. In 1308, he and a large team of assistants were working in Naples cathedral. Cavallini was instrumental in the renewal of Roman painting. Turning his back on Byzantine tradition, he concentrated on creating rounded, three-dimensional figures and on using colour in a realistic way.

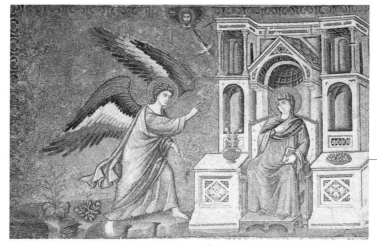

♦ **ANNUNCIATION**
A detail from Pietro Cavallini's mosaics of the Life of the Virgin, Santa Maria in Trastevere, Rome, c.1291. The splendid golden background does not overpower the figures. They appear realistically three-dimensional, and this is achieved by Cavallini's sensitive use of colour.

♦ **SUPERVISION**
Pietro Cavallini supervised the progress of the mosaic from above.

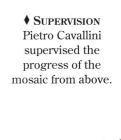

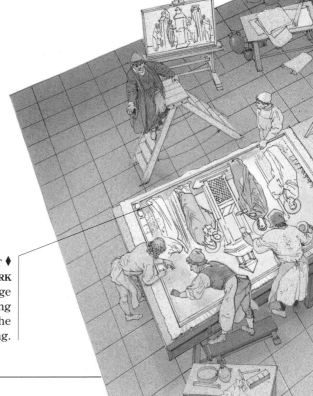

♦ **SERAPH**
A detail from Pietro Cavallini's *Last Judgement,* Santa Maria in Trastevere, Rome. Emerging from the layer of wings, the face of the seraph is rendered in lively colours with subtle gradations of tone.

**MOSAICISTS AT ♦ WORK**
Craftsmen arrange the *tesserae* following the outlines of the master's drawing.

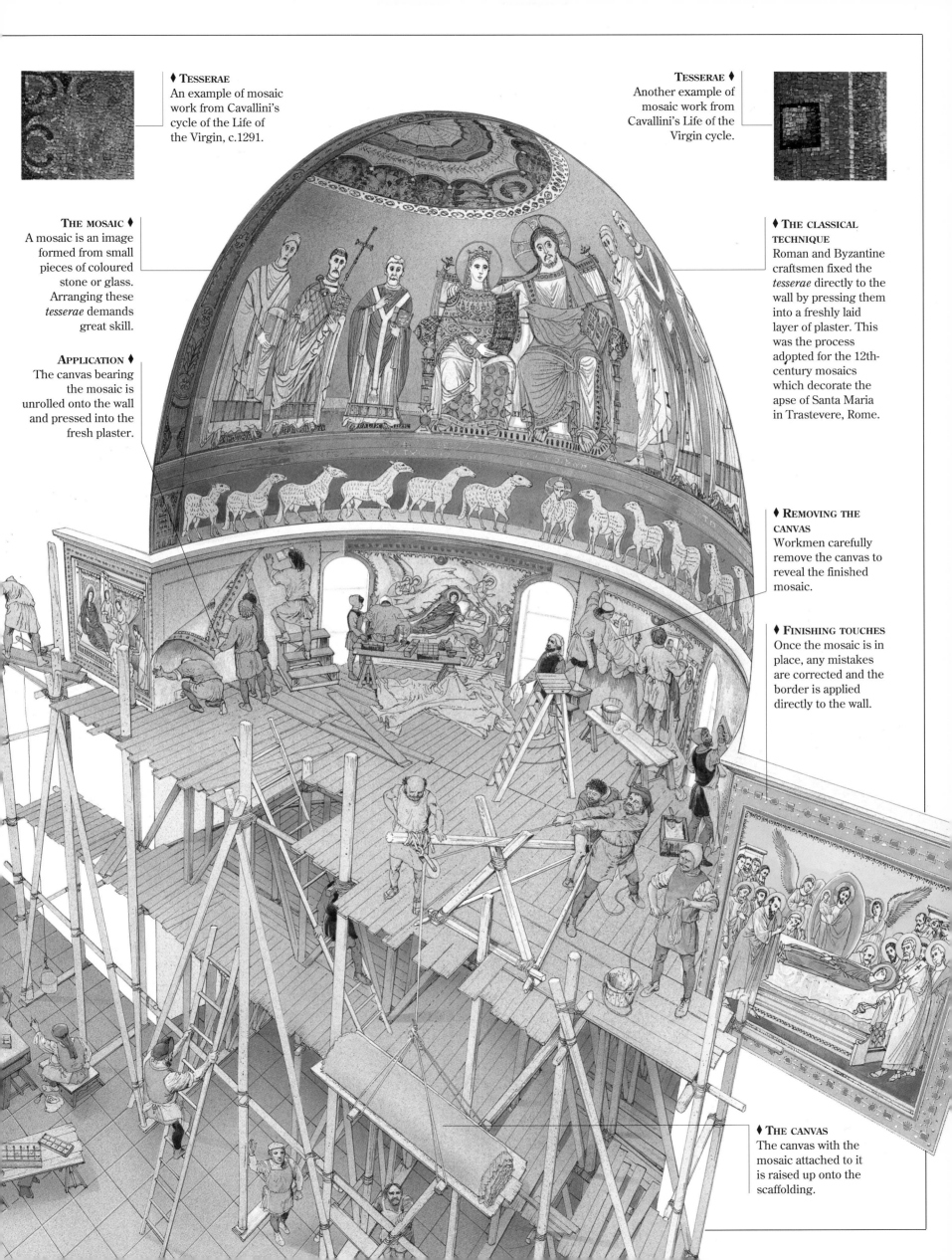

♦ TESSERAE
An example of mosaic work from Cavallini's cycle of the Life of the Virgin, c.1291.

TESSERAE ♦
Another example of mosaic work from Cavallini's Life of the Virgin cycle.

THE MOSAIC ♦
A mosaic is an image formed from small pieces of coloured stone or glass. Arranging these *tesserae* demands great skill.

APPLICATION ♦
The canvas bearing the mosaic is unrolled onto the wall and pressed into the fresh plaster.

♦ THE CLASSICAL TECHNIQUE
Roman and Byzantine craftsmen fixed the *tesserae* directly to the wall by pressing them into a freshly laid layer of plaster. This was the process adopted for the 12th-century mosaics which decorate the apse of Santa Maria in Trastevere, Rome.

♦ REMOVING THE CANVAS
Workmen carefully remove the canvas to reveal the finished mosaic.

♦ FINISHING TOUCHES
Once the mosaic is in place, any mistakes are corrected and the border is applied directly to the wall.

♦ THE CANVAS
The canvas with the mosaic attached to it is raised up onto the scaffolding.

# THE LAST JUDGEMENT

Giotto was commissioned to paint frescos in the Scrovegni Chapel in Padua, which is also known as the Arena Chapel. Enrico Scrovegni, who commissioned him, was having the chapel built as a way of expiating the sins of his father, a usurer. The concepts of sin, judgement and expiation were central to late medieval painting. Christians believed that, at the end of history, Christ would return to earth, the dead would rise from their graves, and there would be a final reckoning. All men would be judged according to their deeds and sent to either Heaven or Hell. After the year 1000, the Church made the Last Judgement a central theme of its preaching. It was the chief subject of late Romanesque sculpture in France, often depicted in the lunettes over church doors. In Italy, it was more often illustrated in murals (mosaics and frescos), or sculpted on church pulpits. In the upper part of a work of this kind, Christ was portrayed as supreme Judge, enthroned or on a rainbow, and flanked by the apostles. In the lower part, the dead were shown rising from their graves; in the centre, the archangel Michael held a balance for weighing souls, while the Virgin interceded for those appearing before the throne of judgement.

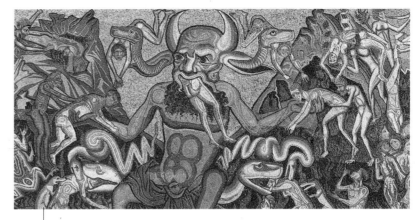

♦ **INFERNO**
A detail from a *Last Judgement* by Coppo di Marcovaldo (b. c.1225) in the Baptistery, Florence. The devil, depicted as a monster, seems to draw the damned souls into his clutches. Their despair is conveyed in their expressions and gestures.

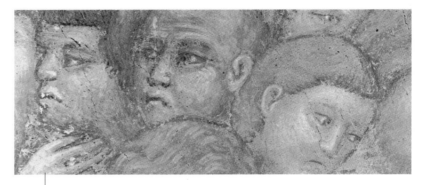

♦ **PIETRO CAVALLINI**
*Last Judgement*, part of Cavallini's fresco cycle for Santa Cecilia in Trastevere, Rome. Whereas the figures in the *Last Judgement* at Torcello are packed together, here they are arranged in horizontal lines, creating an atmosphere of serenity and balance.

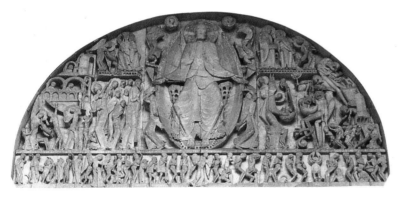

♦ **THE LAST JUDGEMENT**
A Romanesque sculpture at Autun cathedral, France, from the first half of the 12th century. This *Last Judgement* was located in the tympanum above the main door of the cathedral. It gave food for thought: what might the believer expect in the afterlife? The extreme distortion and visionary quality of Romanesque sculpture add to the sense of the horrors awaiting sinners who do not repent.

**10 ♦ GIOTTO'S LIFE STORY.** *The fresco cycle in the Arena Chapel at Padua is considered to be Giotto's greatest work in terms of complexity and artistic maturity. It was commissioned in 1302 by Enrico Scrovegni, then the richest citizen of Padua, for a private chapel that he was having built. According to a Paduan chronicler writing in the 16th century, Scrovegni's intention in building this private chapel dedicated to the Virgin was to atone for the sins of his father, Reginaldo, who was a notorious usurer (money-lender) – a reputation which won him a place among the damned souls of Dante's* Divine Comedy. *Giotto himself must have been sensitive about this issue: as a rich and clever businessman, he had practised similar forms of exploitation, hiring out looms at exorbitant rates to the poor weavers of Florence.* ≫→

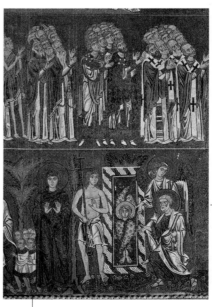

♦ **TORCELLO CATHEDRAL**
This mosaic at Torcello cathedral, dating from the early 12th century, is one of the finest examples of a *Last Judgement* in the Byzantine style. Typical Byzantine features are the set group consisting of Christ, the Virgin and St John the Baptist, the symbolic representation of the throne on which the supreme Judge is to sit, and the River of Fire which sweeps the damned off to hell. All of these were elements which were no longer found in Romanesque or Gothic art.

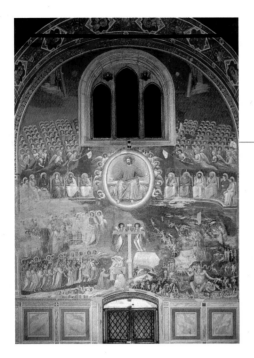

♦ GIOTTO
*Last Judgement*, Scrovegni Chapel, Padua, 1302-6. The elements which make up Giotto's fresco are the traditional ones used in representations of the Last Judgement, but they are arranged in an original way.

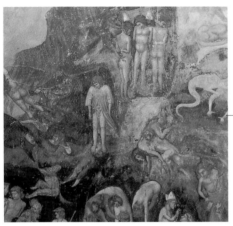

♦ THE DAMNED
A detail from Giotto's *Last Judgement*. Representations of hell showed the punishments inflicted on lost souls. The figure of Judas, who hanged himself, is often given prominence.

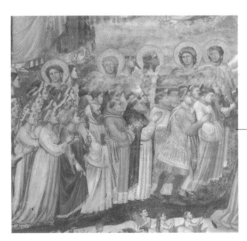

♦ THE ELECT
Those people who are saved are shown entering Paradise, guided by the archangel Michael. A detail from Giotto's *Last Judgement*.

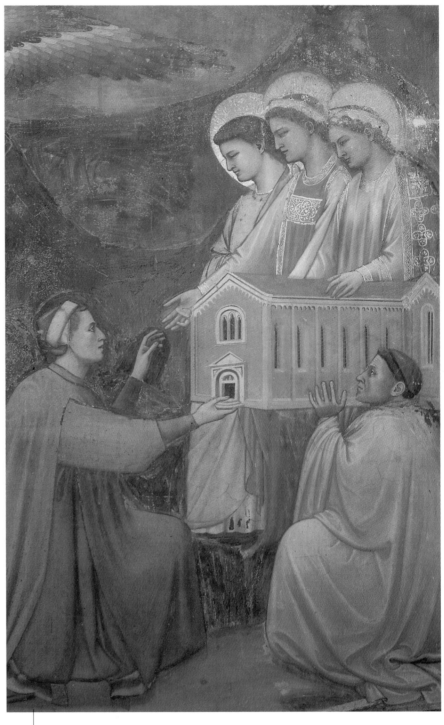

♦ ENRICO SCROVEGNI
A detail from Giotto's *Last Judgement*. Enrico Scrovegni, on the side of the elect, kneels before the Virgin Mary and offers a model of the chapel building by which he hoped to earn merit in heaven. Atoning for one's sins, by good works or by suffering the fires of Purgatory, was a subject that obsessed many people in the Middle Ages.

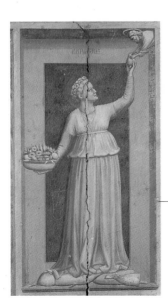
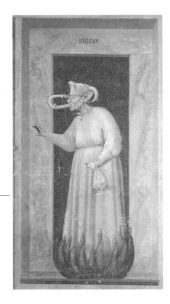

♦ USURY
The subject of usury plays a central part in the decoration of the chapel. Figures representing the vices and virtues are painted in the lower bands on the side walls. Charity is not paired with Avarice but with Envy, who is shown grasping her purse (normally an attribute of Avarice). This can be interpreted as the lust for riches.

Another novel feature is the unusual prominence given to the scene (reproduced on the right) of the priests paying Judas to betray Jesus. The apostle who sold Jesus for financial gain is also depicted holding a purse. Behind him stands the devil. This is the only episode in the whole of the fresco cycle in which the devil appears.

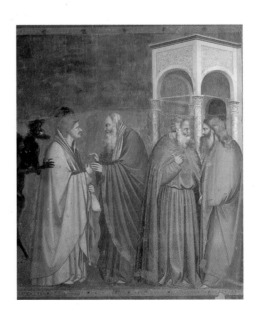

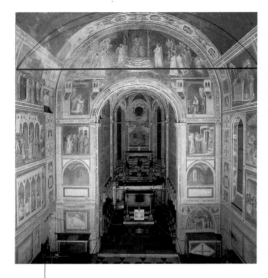

◆ **FROM THE ENTRANCE**
A view of the triumphal arch.

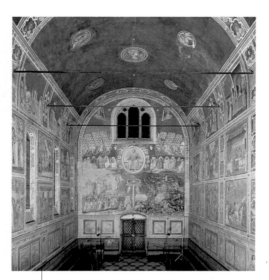

◆ **FROM THE ALTAR**
A view of the *Last Judgement*.

# THE SCROVEGNI CHAPEL, PADUA

The chapel is of modest proportions, roughly 13 metres long, 8.5 metres wide and 13 metres high (43 x 30 x 43 feet). It is also very simple in design: a rectangular structure of red brick, its roof a single barrel vault. But the internal walls are decorated from floor to ceiling with Giotto's most famous fresco cycle. Arranged in three horizontal bands, the paintings depict the story of Joachim and Anna (Mary's parents), the life of the Virgin, and the life of Christ until the time of Pentecost. Also represented are the ancestors of Christ, kings and members of the tribe of Judah, prophets (in the medallions on the ceiling), and of course the great *Last Judgement*, which takes up the whole of the entrance wall. The cycle is a magnificent demonstration of Giotto's mastery of space and colour.

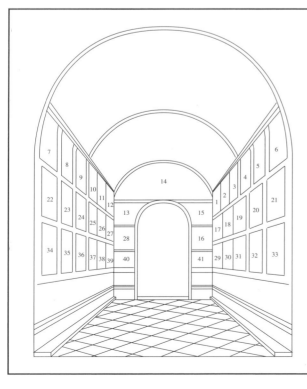

The scenes in the upper band tell the stories of Joachim and Anna (panels 1-6) and of their daughter Mary (7-12), while the upper part of the triumphal arch supports the *Annunciation* (13-15). The two lower bands are devoted to the story of the life of Christ (16-39) which is concluded with the images of two small vaulted chambers (40- 41) on the end wall. At ground level, between imitation marble panels, are Virtues (right) and Vices (left).

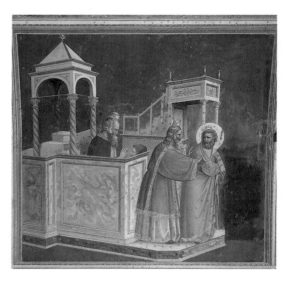

◆ **THE EXPULSION OF JOACHIM**
Giotto begins the story with the scene of Joachim being expelled from the temple. His fault is that he has failed to produce children (Panel 1).

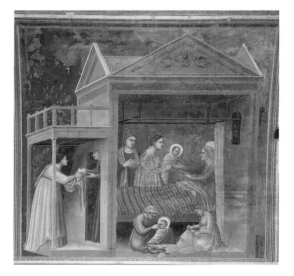

◆ **MARY'S BIRTH**
The long-awaited moment arrives: in the room where she received the angel's message, Anna gives birth to Mary, the one whom God has chosen to be Jesus's mother (Panel 7).

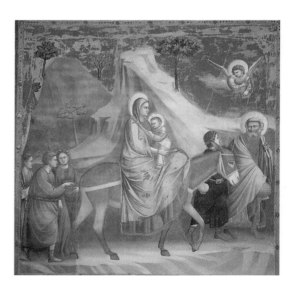

◆ **THE FLIGHT INTO EGYPT**
Some time after the birth of Jesus, the family flees to Egypt. Herod, King of Judah, seeks to kill the child and has ordered that all under two be put to death (Panel 20).

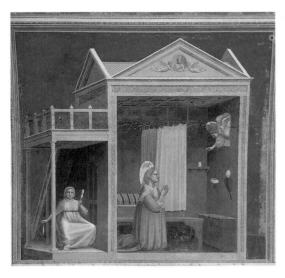

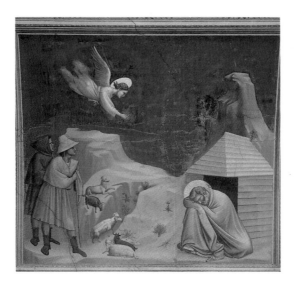

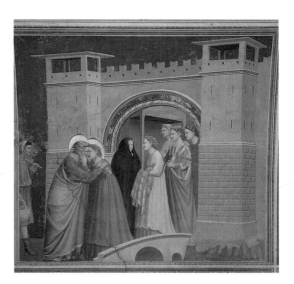

♦ **THE ANNUNCIATION TO ANNA**
However, at home one day, Joachim's wife Anna is visited by an angel bearing good tidings: it will soon be her turn to rejoice in the birth of a child (Panel 3).

♦ **THE DREAM OF JOACHIM**
An angel also informs Joachim of the news. Joachim receives the message in a dream, after going away to pray and do penance among the shepherds (Panel 5).

♦ **THE MEETING AT THE GOLDEN GATE**
At last Joachim is able to return to Jerusalem, and he meets his wife at the Golden Gate. She welcomes him with signs of warm affection (Panel 6).

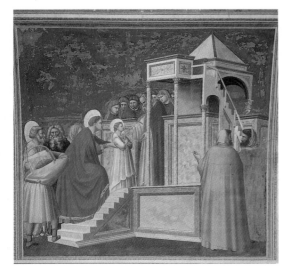

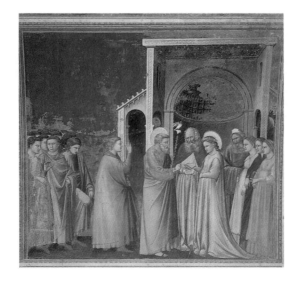

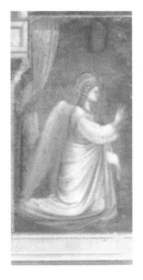
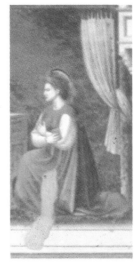

♦ **THE PRESENTATION OF MARY**
While she is still a child, Mary is presented to the priests in the temple. Not many years later, her son Jesus will go through the same ceremony (Panel 8).

♦ **THE BETROTHAL OF THE VIRGIN**
Mary is betrothed to Joseph, a carpenter from Nazareth. His task will be to care for Mary and act as earthly father to the Son of God (Panel 11).

♦ **THE ANNUNCIATION**
Sent by God, the archangel Gabriel tells Mary that she will give birth to Jesus. Gabriel is depicted on the left of the triumphal arch and Mary on the right (Panels 13 and 15).

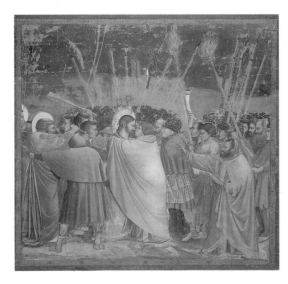

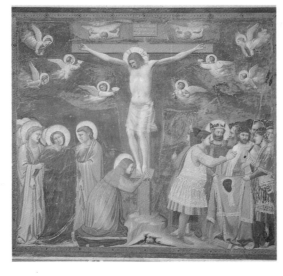

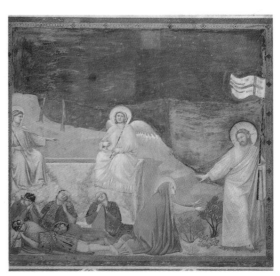

♦ **THE ARREST OF JESUS**
Some thirty years later, betrayed by Judas, Jesus is arrested by Roman soldiers. Judas has arranged with them that he will kiss the man whom they should arrest (Panel 31).

♦ **THE CRUCIFIXION**
Jesus is put on trial, found guilty and condemned to death by crucifixion. He undergoes hours of terrible suffering on the cross before giving up his spirit (Panel 35).

♦ **THE RESURRECTION**
Three days after the Friday of his death, it is found that Jesus's body has disappeared from the tomb. Jesus has risen and will soon take his place beside his Father in heaven (Panel 39).

# GIOTTO'S ORIGINALITY

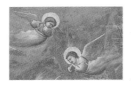

**♦ ANGELS**
A detail from the *Lamentation over Christ's body*, in the Scrovegni Chapel, 1302-6. Angels hover in the sky, apparently beside themselves with grief. Uttering cries of sorrow, they swoop and soar on bird-like wings.

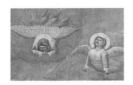

**♦ GIOTTO'S PAINTING**
Giotto brought a naturalism into his painting that was totally unprecedented in medieval art. The rhythm of his narrative, as in the scene of the *Lamentation*, is always calm and dignified. The emotional tension arises from the subtle differentiation of features, expressions and attitudes, and also from the way in which Giotto uses line and colour to concentrate attention on the content and significance of an event. Giotto does everything he can to represent the story in a realistic, effective way. He takes into account even apparently secondary details, and his extraordinary ability to create on a flat surface a sense of depth and relationships between his figures and objects makes his works seem even more tangible and convincing.

A particular characteristic of Giotto's painting is the way he represented spiritual and supernatural subjects in warm, human, earthly terms. In earlier painting, and particularly in Byzantine art, the Madonna was represented as the austere queen of heaven. In the *Nativity* scene in the Scrovegni Chapel, Giotto shows her as a gentle mother, tenderly reaching out to embrace her baby. Only the expression in her eyes seems not to accord with her maternal gesture: it communicates an awareness of the momentous events her son is to experience when he grows up.

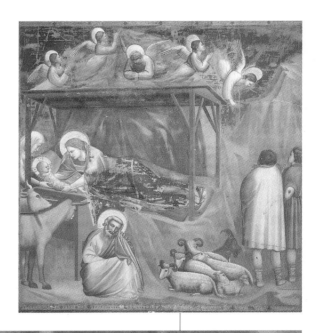

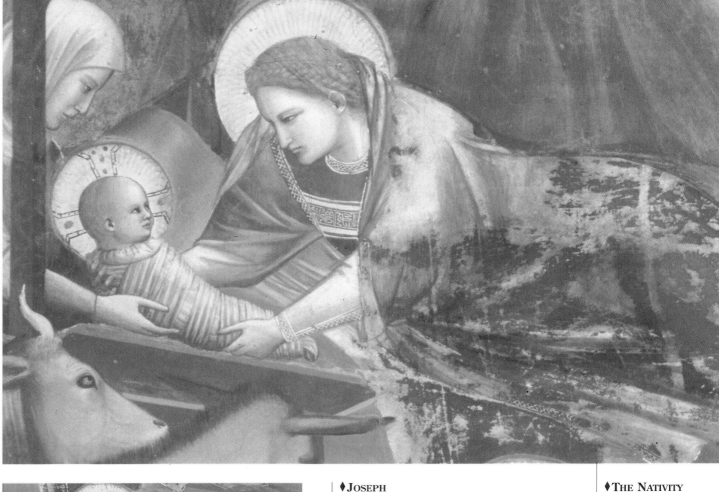

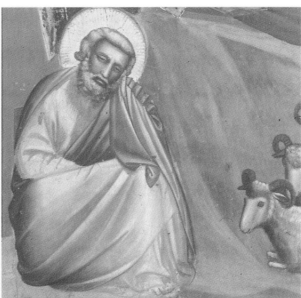

**♦ JOSEPH**
A detail from the *Nativity,* Scrovegni Chapel, 1302-6. The figure of Joseph, seated in the foreground, conveys a feeling of great serenity and restfulness. With his head on his hand and his eyes half closing, he seems to be on the point of falling asleep.

**♦ THE NATIVITY**
A detail (above) and the whole (top) of the *Nativity.* As well as the birth of Christ, the painting shows, on the right, the angels announcing the news of Jesus's birth to the shepherds. The two elements of the story co-exist perfectly. A physical link is provided by the group of sheep and goats, some looking towards the manger scene and some towards the shepherds.

The *Lamentation* is one of the most moving scenes Giotto painted in the Scrovegni Chapel. The Madonna, the apostles and the angels, who surround the body of Christ, now brought down from the cross, are all participating in the scene. The drama is staged in a dignified way, with nothing exaggerated or out of place. Gestures are restrained, expressions of grief subdued. The characters are not shown taking any particular action, but rather they express a sense of deeply-felt inner pain. The dramatic tension, culminating in the faces of the Madonna and of Christ, is emphasized by the rhythm of the colours and shapes. All the paintings in the Scrovegni Chapel were done in the period from 1302 to 1306.

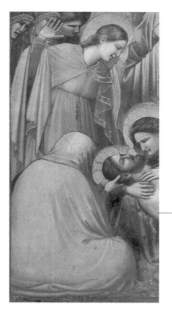

◆ **SEEN FROM BEHIND**
A detail from the *Lamentation*. Giotto often painted figures with their backs to the spectator, thereby creating a sense of depth and space. In addition, these figures seen from behind are sharing the view that we, the spectators, have of the main scene. We identify with them and, in this way, they serve to involve us in the picture.

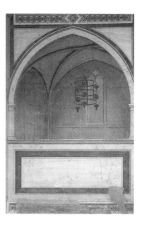

◆ **ILLUSIONS**
*Vaulted chambers*, two panels from the lowest band of frescos on the wall of the triumphal arch of the Scrovegni Chapel. Giotto painted two small chambers with cross-vaults and Gothic windows. This was the first time that an artist had used perspective in this way. Giotto's mastery in depicting three-dimensional space is evident above all in details such as the way he has used the imitation marble panelling below his paintings of two vaulted chambers, to create a complete optical illusion of two small rooms. Giotto did not use this kind of illusion in the biblical scenes he painted, but only on parts of the walls where they would seem like additions to the actual internal architecture of the chapel. So he created an illusion of space in two ways: the illusion of real space into which we feel we could walk; and the sense of space and depth within each scene of the story.

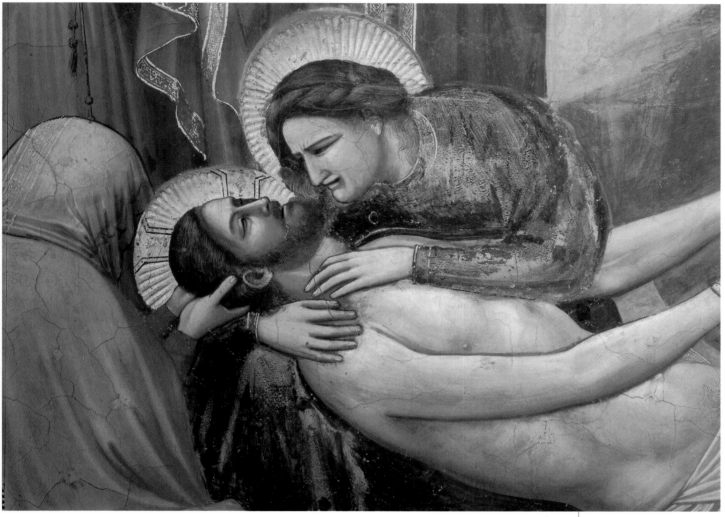

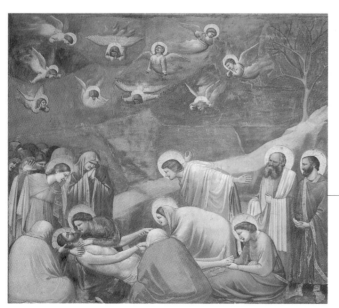

◆ **BALANCE**
The whole panel of the *Lamentation*. Giotto creates a sense of balance by his arrangement of solid shapes: the rocky hillside, the bending figure of St John, the kneeling woman, the two figures sitting beside the body of Christ. This balance is reinforced by his use of graduated colour: from the more transparent colours in the foreground to the vivid colours of the angels.

◆ **CHRIST AND THE MADONNA**
A detail from the *Lamentation*. The heads of the mother and son are the focal point of the scene. To concentrate the spectator's attention, Giotto has painted all his characters looking inwards towards this spot. The same purpose is served by the diagonal lines of the rocky hillside and the strong vertical lines of the figures standing on the right.

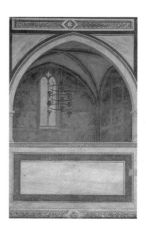

# In Santa Croce

The frescos Giotto painted for the Bardi and Peruzzi chapels in the church of Santa Croce in Florence mark a further development in his efforts to produce a coherent, convincing representation of space. Thinking of the viewpoint of the spectator standing on the threshold, he represented architectural features from an appropriate angle and painted figures and buildings as if the light source were the real windows of the chapel. The overall effect is one of monumental spaciousness, achieved not by a knowledge of linear perspective, the mathematical principles of which were not systematically practised until the 15th century, but as a result of a new concern to reproduce reality.

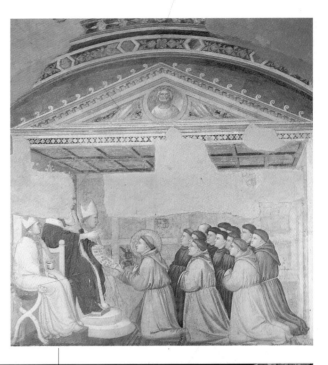

Giotto's workshop in Florence continued to produce works of major importance in response to commissions from Pisa, Padua and Bologna. From 1315 to 1325, frescos were painted for the Bardi and Peruzzi chapels in the Florentine church of Santa Croce. Though signed by Giotto, many of these works were inevitably executed by his assistants. Giotto was, in this respect, the first artist entrepreneur: responsible for the conception and supervision of a work, but not for its implementation. Giotto's reputation was now widely established and the great rulers of the day competed for his services. In the last years of his life, he travelled continually up and down Italy. Nevertheless, Florence remained the focus of his activity, and the flourishing workshop he had established there represented continuity. Even in his absence, his assistants were able to get on with the work in hand. In Florence, Giotto's main concern was the fresco cycles for the church of Santa Croce, where he had undertaken to decorate four chapels. Parts of only two of these cycles have survived. In the Peruzzi chapel there are frescos of scenes from the lives of St John the Baptist and St John the Evangelist, which were painted between 1315 and 1320. In the Bardi chapel there are frescos of some scenes of the Life of St Francis (c.1325). Both chapels are situated in the transept of Santa Croce and are named after the Florentine banking families who commissioned the works.

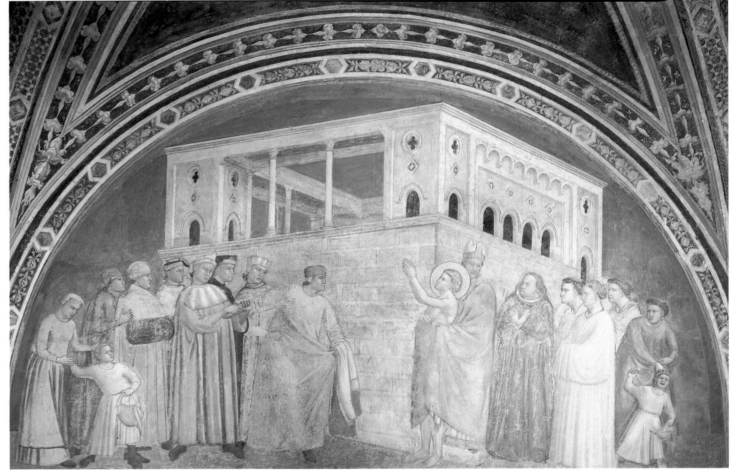

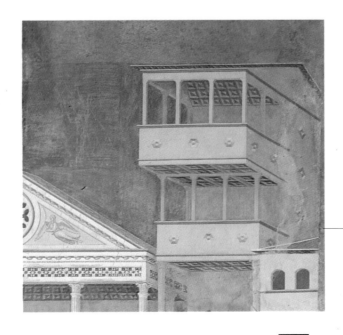

**♦ THE EARLIER WORK**
A detail from a Giotto's *Francis renouncing his earthly possessions,* Upper Church, Assisi.

**♦ SETTING THE SCENE**
In his frescos for the Bardi chapel in Santa Croce, Giotto represented scenes from the Life of St Francis which he had already painted at Assisi. But the settings of the Florentine paintings are more simple and effective. For instance, in the scene of *Francis renouncing his earthly possessions* (above), the sharp angle of the building concentrates attention on the figure of the saint and underlines the contrast between the two opposing groups. Top right is a detail from the *Confirmation of the Rule*.

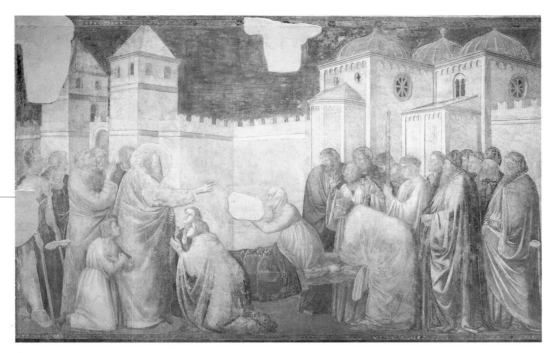

THE RAISING OF ◆
DRUSIANA
A fresco painted by
Giotto in the Peruzzi
chapel, Santa Croce,
Florence, 1315-20.
This is the first
instance in which
Giotto has not
confined the
buildings in the scene
strictly within the
picture space. They
have not been kept
rigidly within the
frame, but look as if
they extend beyond it
on either side. The
effect is more
naturalistic.

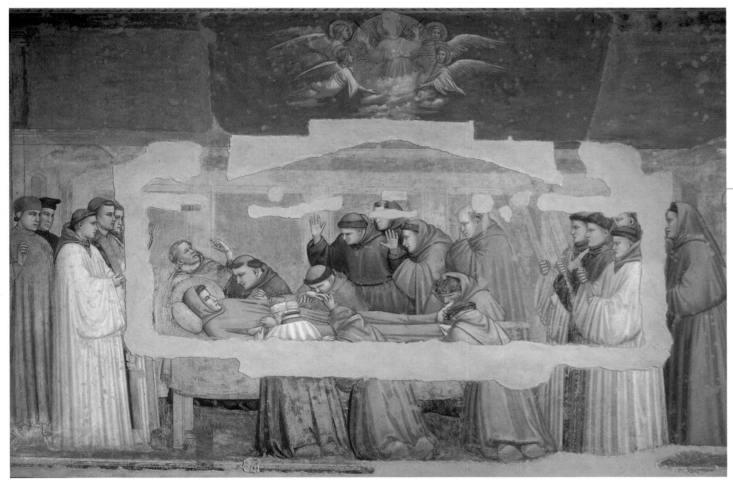

◆ VERIFICATION OF
THE STIGMATA
A fresco by Giotto in
the Bardi chapel,
1315-20. This scene
combines two
episodes which
Giotto had depicted
separately at Assisi:
the Death of St
Francis and the
Verification of the
stigmata. In this later
work, details of the
architectural setting
are kept to a
minimum. The scene
is one of the most
impressively moving
that Giotto ever
painted.

BROTHERLY LOVE ◆
A detail from the
fresco of the
*Verification of the
stigmata*, Bardi
chapel, Santa Croce,
Florence, 1350-20.
There is neither
exaggeration nor
awkwardness in this
picture of the friars
expressing their
grief. Giotto captured
their feelings of
tenderness and
affection in a realistic
way that had never
been achieved by
earlier artists.

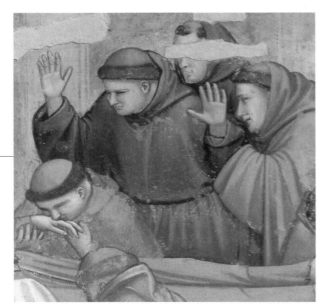

**11 ◆ GIOTTO'S LIFE STORY.** *In medieval times, the artist was usually considered little more than an artisan, but with Giotto his social status began to change. Giotto's work was held in such high regard that when he was serving Robert of Anjou, in Naples, the king made him a member of his household, and two years later granted him a pension. From 1328 to 1333, Giotto and a large team of assistants worked at the Neapolitan court. Next to nothing has survived from those years: a fresco fragment of the* Lamentation *(Nuns' Cloister, Santa Chiara, Naples), another very poorly preserved fresco of the* Miracle of the Loaves and Fishes *(Chapter House, Santa Chiara) and some heads of* Saints *and* Famous Men *in the chapel of Santa Barbara at Castelnuovo. Giotto ran a workshop in Naples, as well as Florence, with many assistants under him.* ⮕

# GIOTTO AS ARCHITECT

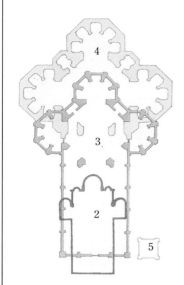

By 1330, a programme to enlarge and improve the city of Florence, begun fifty years earlier, was drawing to a close. Under the supervision of the sculptor and architect Arnolfo di Cambio, the new city walls, the Palazzo dei Priori and the Palazzo Vecchio had been completed, and new streets and squares laid out. It only remained to finish work on the new cathedral of Santa Maria del Fiore. The plan, initiated in 1296 by Arnolfo di Cambio, was to replace the old Romanesque cathedral of Santa Reparata, now outgrown, with a church more appropriate to the increasing prestige of Florence and its rapidly expanding population. The new façade was quickly completed and in 1334 Giotto, as the greatest living artist, was appointed architect to the cathedral. In the last three years of his life, he planned and began building the bell tower (campanile), but it was not finished until after his death, in 1357.

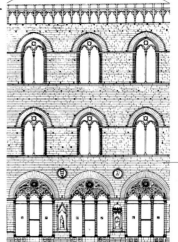

♦ LOGGIA
In 1337, the year Giotto died, work began on the loggia of Orsanmichele, which served as a corn exchange. Further floors were added to the building and these were used as a public granary.

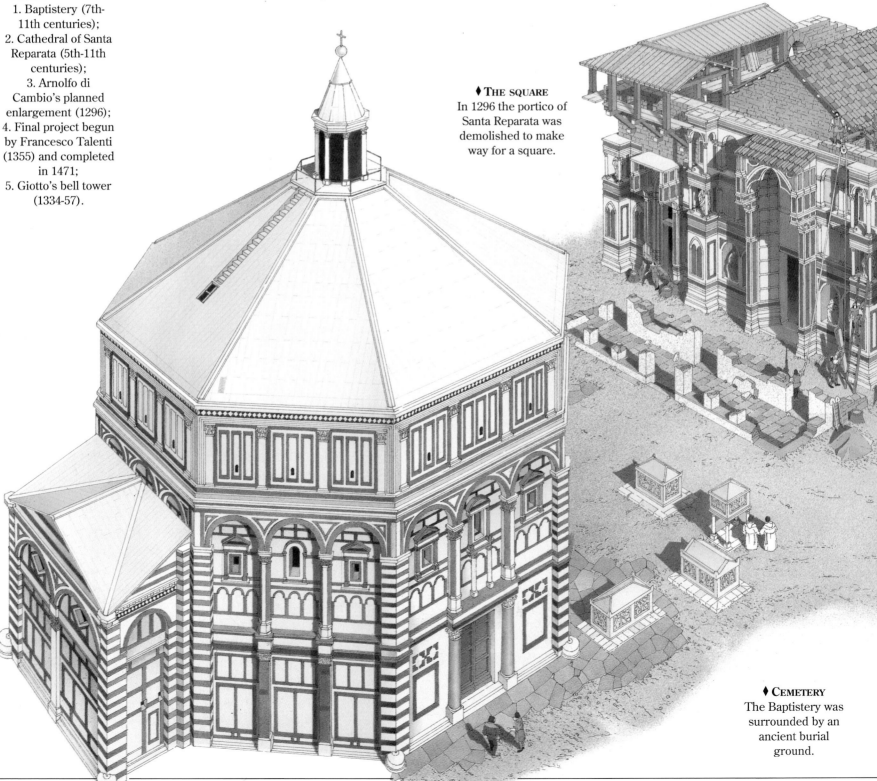

♦ THE SQUARE
In 1296 the portico of Santa Reparata was demolished to make way for a square.

♦ CEMETERY
The Baptistery was surrounded by an ancient burial ground.

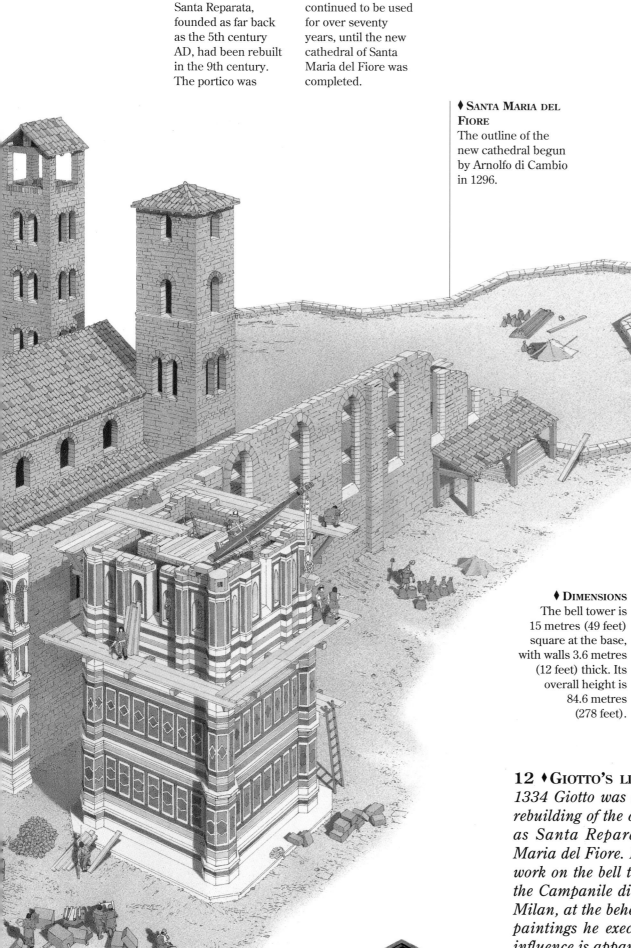

♦ TRANSITION
The old cathedral of Santa Reparata, founded as far back as the 5th century AD, had been rebuilt in the 9th century. The portico was demolished, but the old building continued to be used for over seventy years, until the new cathedral of Santa Maria del Fiore was completed.

♦ SANTA MARIA DEL FIORE
The outline of the new cathedral begun by Arnolfo di Cambio in 1296.

THE BELL TOWER ♦
According to Giotto's original plan, the campanile should have culminated in a tall spire. This feature was suppressed by Francesco Talenti.

♦ DIMENSIONS
The bell tower is 15 metres (49 feet) square at the base, with walls 3.6 metres (12 feet) thick. Its overall height is 84.6 metres (278 feet).

DECORATION ♦
*The Art of Building*, one of twenty-one relief panels that were sculpted by Andrea Pisano and his assistants before 1342, to decorate the lower part of Giotto's bell tower (Museo dell'Opera del Duomo).

**12 ♦ GIOTTO'S LIFE STORY.** *Back in Florence again, in 1334 Giotto was appointed as architect to supervise the rebuilding of the city's cathedral church, formerly known as Santa Reparata and now to be known as Santa Maria del Fiore. He was responsible for the first phase of work on the bell tower, which is now named after him – the Campanile di Giotto. From 1334 to 1336 he was in Milan, at the behest of the city's ruler, Azzo Visconti. The paintings he executed there have not survived, but his influence is apparent in the work of Lombard artists who met him and saw his work at this time. Giotto always left a deep impression, revolutionizing the practice of local schools of painting. This had been true in Umbria, Rimini, Padua, Rome and Naples, and of course in Tuscany, where artists had taken on board his innovations, albeit adapting them to their own ends. Giotto died at the age of seventy on 8 January 1337 and was buried with all due ceremony in the cathedral.*

# A NEW STYLE

Many of the greatest artists – Leonardo or Michelangelo, Rembrandt or Goya, for instance – are not regarded as having started a school of painting. Giotto did. He directly influenced the work of his pupils, many of whom became major artists in their own right, and he was instrumental in determining the style of following generations. By the time of Giotto's death, there had been a radical change in the prevailing style of painting. His work spelled an end to the stylization of Byzantine art. He introduced naturalism in art, in the representation of people and objects with real depth, and this opened the way for the Renaissance. The work of Giotto and his followers in the 14th century therefore marks a major turning point in the history of European art.

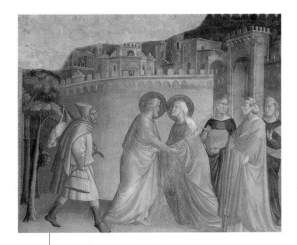

♦ **ADORATION OF THE SHEPHERDS**
A fresco by Taddeo Gaddi in the Baroncelli chapel, Santa Croce, Florence, 1332-38.

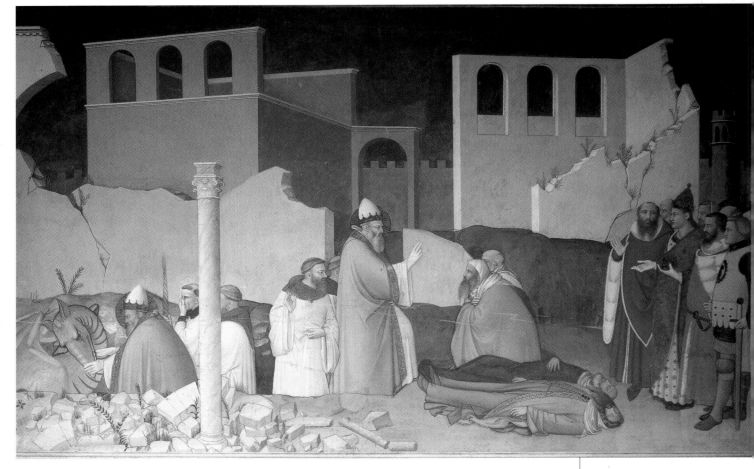

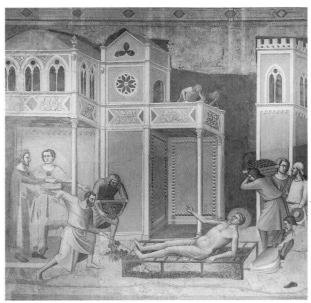

♦ **THE MARTYRDOM OF ST LAWRENCE**
A fresco painted by Bernardo Daddi in the Pulci chapel, Santa Croce, Florence, c.1330. This dramatic scene includes some telling details such as the men placing charcoal under the grille on which the saint lies and the man working the bellows to fan the fire.

♦ **ST SYLVESTER RAISES TWO MAGICIANS**
A fresco by Maso di Banco in the Bardi di Vernio chapel, Santa Croce, Florence (1340- 45). The debt to Giotto is clear. However, Maso also demonstrates an ability to innovate in his Santa Croce frescos.

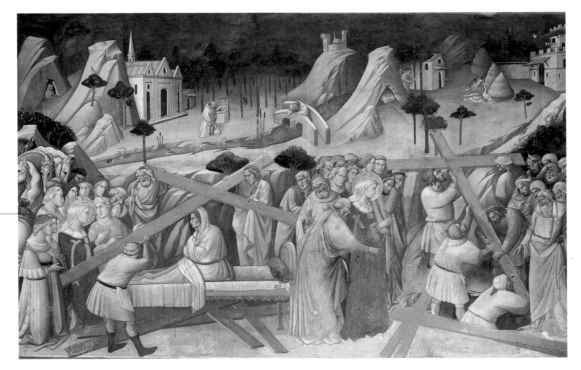

**DISCOVERY OF THE ♦ TRUE CROSS**
A fresco painted by Agnolo Gaddi in Santa Croce, Florence, 1380-85. In his frescos, the artist gives free rein to his story-telling abilities. The composition is typical of Giotto. Within this, Gaddi has included anecdotal details, such as the monk in the background who is watching the water run under the bridge, and landscapes of obvious Gothic inspiration.

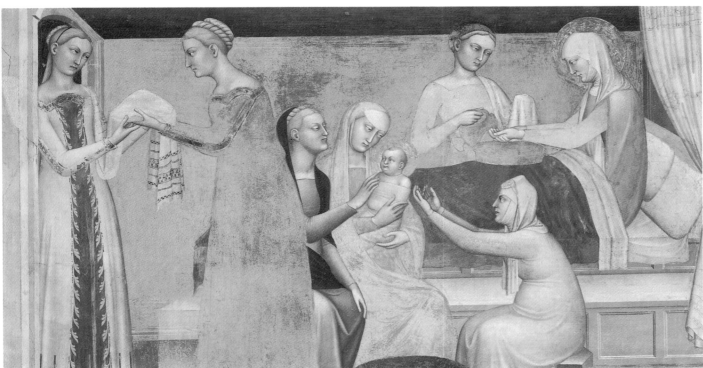

**THE BIRTH OF THE ♦ VIRGIN**
A detail of a fresco painted by Giovanni da Milano in the Rinuccini chapel, Santa Croce, Florence, 1365. Giovanni covers large areas with a range of vivid colours.

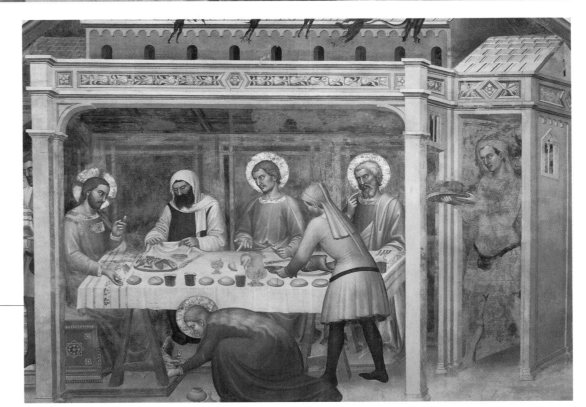

**CHRIST IN THE ♦ PHARISEE'S HOUSE**
A detail of a fresco by Giovanni da Milano, in the Rinuccini chapel, Santa Croce, Florence, 1365.

**♦ GIOTTO'S FOLLOWERS IN SANTA CROCE**
The Franciscan church of Santa Croce in Florence, where Giotto painted his last masterpieces, contains work by almost all of the master's local pupils and followers. Taddeo Gaddi painted frescos of scenes from the Life of the Virgin for the Baroncelli chapel (1332-38). After 1330, Bernardo Daddi decorated the Pulci chapel with stories of St Lawrence and St Stephen. From 1340, Maso di Banco worked in the Bardi di Vernio chapel on frescos depicting the life of St Sylvester. Agnolo Gaddi, last heir to the Giottesque tradition, decorated the Castellani chapel with stories of anchorites (religious hermits) and, in the choir, painted the *Legend of the true cross* (1380-85).

Top, the façade of Santa Croce; below, a view inside the Baroncelli chapel.

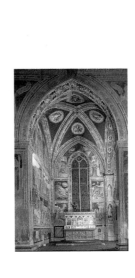

# SIENESE PAINTING

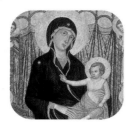

♦ **THE RUCELLAI MADONNA**
Duccio, 1285 (Uffizi Gallery, Florence). A central detail showing St Zenobius.

♦ **DUCCIO DI BUONINSEGNA**
(Siena, c.1260-1318/19).
The earliest mention of Duccio is in connection with some decorative work he did for the city council of Siena in 1278. We know nothing of his training as a painter, but in 1285 he was commissioned to paint the *Rucellai Madonna*, an altar-piece for the church of Santa Maria Novella in Florence. Because of similarities between this work and comparable paintings by Cimabue, art historians believe that Duccio may have been a pupil of the Florentine master.

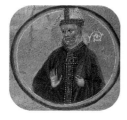

However, Duccio, who was influenced by the Gothic style of northern Europe, pursued a different course from Cimabue. Whereas Cimabue's work surpassed Byzantine art in his concern for depth and facial expression, Duccio's innovations were in his use of line and colour. As well as the *Rucellai Madonna* and *Maestà*, his works include the *Madonna of the Franciscans*. He is considered the leader of the Sienese school.

Duccio di Buoninsegna is considered to be the key figure in the renewal of artistic culture in Siena and the founder of the Sienese school of painting. His position in Siena was similar to that of Giotto in Florence, and he was also influenced by Giotto to a certain extent. Duccio drew from Byzantine art and also from forms of Gothic art, but developed a strong style of his own, conveying human feeling in a realistic way. His example led to further developments in Sienese painting, independent of what was happening elsewhere in Tuscany. Duccio, together with Simone Martini, the Lorenzetti brothers and their various followers, made Siena a major centre of figurative art in Italy in the first half of the early 13th century. It was second only to Florence.

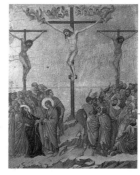

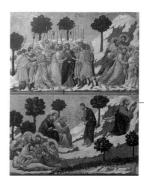

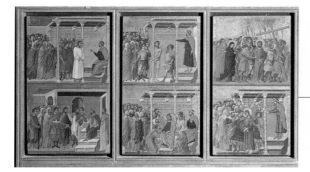

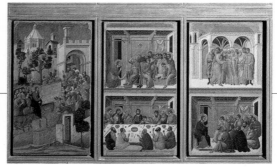

♦ **MAESTÀ**
Duccio di Buoninsegna, tempera on wooden panel, 1311 (Museo dell'Opera del Duomo, Siena). Commissioned in 1308, Duccio's *Maestà* was carried amid popular rejoicing to its place on the high altar of Siena cathedral in 1311. It is painted on both sides. On one, the Madonna is depicted, enthroned and surrounded by saints and angels, against a gold background. The other side consists of fourteen small panels representing the Passion of Christ. Giotto's innovations in conveying volume have been assimilated, but there is little sense of space and depth: the throne appears flat, like an open book. Duccio is less concerned with representing feeling than with using brilliant colour to create a decorative effect.

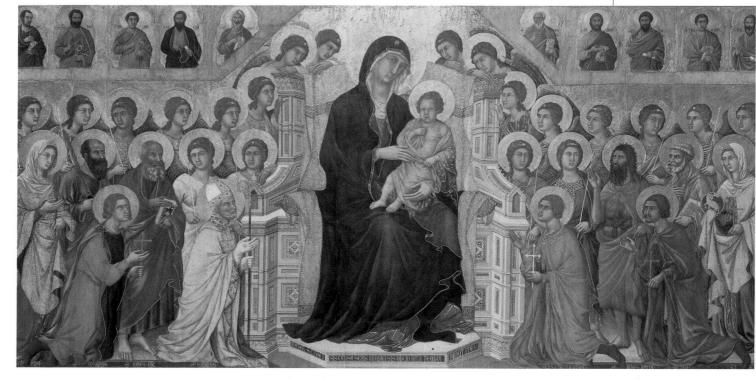

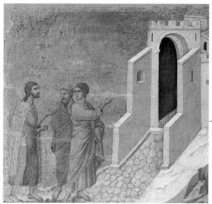

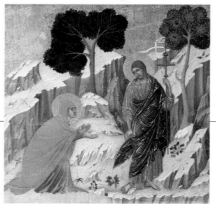

♦ **CHRIST'S PASSION**
Duccio, tempera on wooden panel, 1311 (Museo dell'Opera del Duomo, Siena). These are two of the fourteen scenes depicting the Passion of Christ, which Duccio painted on the reverse of his *Maestà*.

## ♦ SIMONE MARTINI
(Siena, 1284-Avignon, 1344)
Simone was a pupil of Duccio di Buoninsegna. His earliest known work, clearly inspired by French Gothic style, was a *Maestà* for Siena's Palazzo Pubblico (1315). Simone maintained close ties with the Angevin court of Naples, where he painted a panel showing St Louis of Toulouse crowning King Robert. In 1317, Robert dubbed him a knight.

After this, Simone worked at Assisi, painting frescos for the chapel of St Martin, in the Lower Church of St Francis (1320-30). Returning to Siena in 1328, he painted the famous fresco of *Guidoriccio da Fogliano*. In 1336, he moved to Avignon in France, where he was to spend the rest of his life. The frescos he painted there have unfortunately been lost. The most striking characteristic of Simone's art is his use of colour to define space and create atmosphere. His works have an almost fairy-tale character.

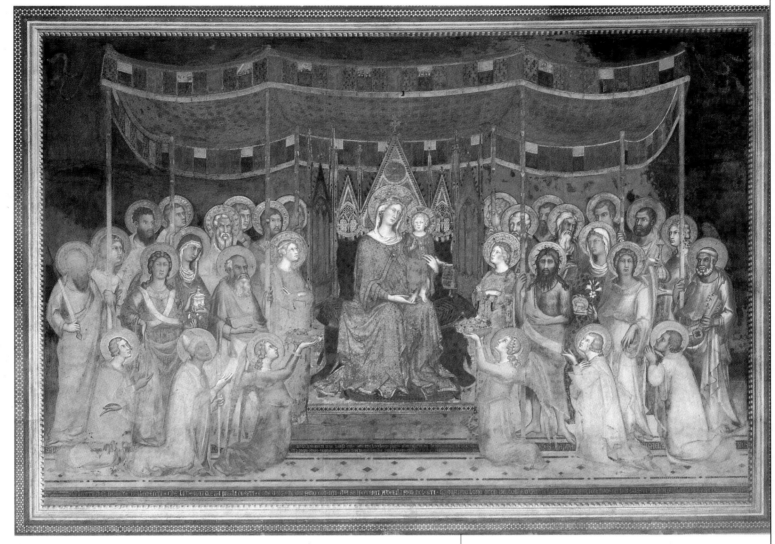

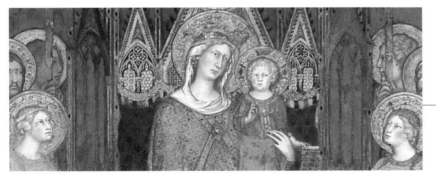

### ♦ MAESTÀ
Simone Martini, 1315 (Palazzo Pubblico, Siena). In this fresco, Simone replaced the traditional golden background with a graceful canopy held up on slim poles. Instead of a heavy marble throne tending to isolate the Madonna, he painted a filigree screen, similar to the setting in which the ladies of a royal court would watch a tournament. The elegant Virgin turns to accept the homage of her admirers.

### GUIDORICCIO DA ♦ FOGLIANO
A fresco by Simone Martini, 1330 (Council Chamber, Palazzo Pubblico, Siena). The fresco depicts Guidoriccio da Fogliano, a successful general, on his way to besiege the town of Montemassi. Painted in vivid colours, the soldier of fortune stands out starkly against the bleak landscape. The curves of the hills echo those of his horse, giving a sense of rhythm to the composition. On the right-hand side there is a camp of tents, among which are two vineyards.

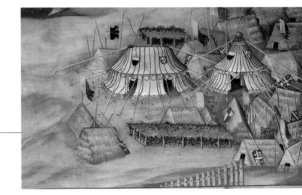

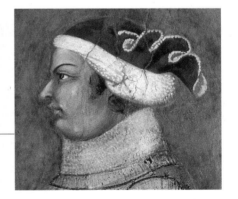

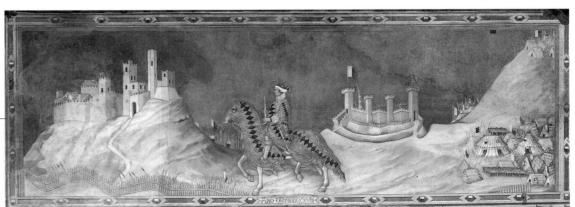

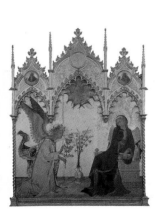

### ♦ ANNUNCIATION
Simone Martini and Lippo Memmi, tempera on wooden panel, 1333 (Uffizi Gallery, Florence).

# THE GOLDEN AGE OF SIENA

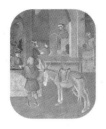

♦ **ALLEGORY OF GOOD GOVERNMENT**
A detail (Palazzo Pubblico, Siena).

♦ **AMBROGIO LORENZETTI**
Ambrogio was born in 1290 and, with his older brother Pietro, is considered one of the great masters of Sienese painting in the 14th century. Although he lived mainly in Siena, he is also known to have made brief visits to Florence. The influence that contemporary Florentine painters had on him is evident in his early interest in the problems of depicting space and volume. This was to remain a constant concern, even when Ambrogio began to concentrate his attention on the use of colour and ways of representing character. His paintings are vibrant, with a sense of gaiety arising from his inclusion of colourful details drawn from everyday life and his evident love of ornament. Ambrogio and Pietro Lorenzetti both died in 1348. They are believed to have been victims of the Black Death, which ravaged both Siena and Florence.

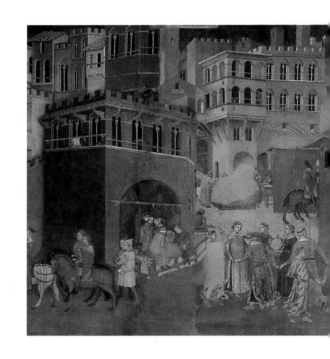

Though only a secondary centre in the early Middle Ages, Siena grew in importance as the Via Franchigena on which it stood became the main traffic artery between Rome, northern Italy and France. The small town expanded, adopting the urban lay-out which survives to this day: the Palazzo Pubblico and civic buildings at its heart, the cathedral set somewhat apart, multi-storied dwellings and workshops lining the narrow, winding streets, the great religious houses on the perimeter and, finally, the imposing circle of walls. In the seventy years up to the plague of 1348, Siena reached the height of its economic power and artistic splendour, rivalling its neighbour, Florence. Siena also produced the first great examples of secular painting, in the work of Ambrogio Lorenzetti.

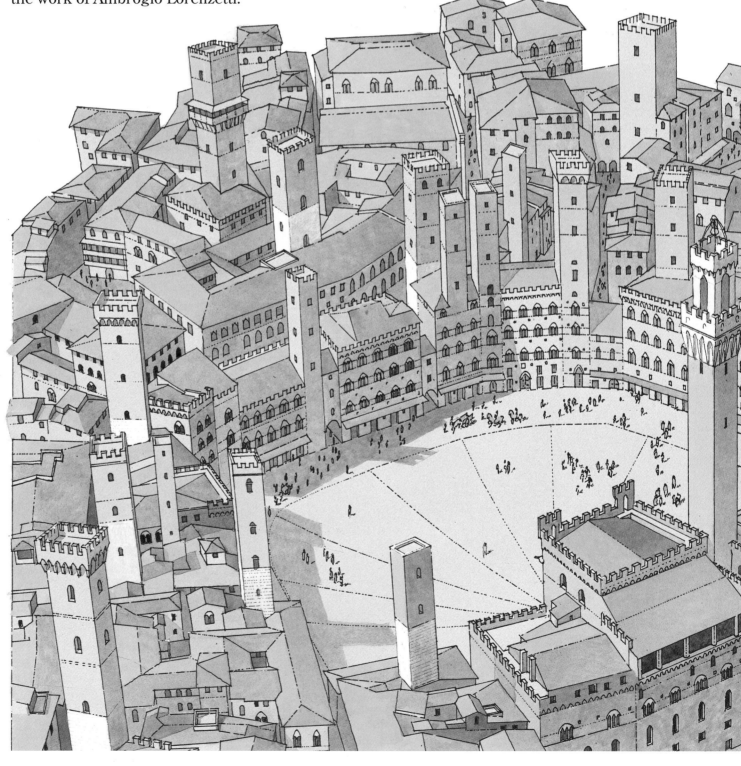

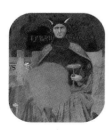

♦ **ALLEGORY OF BAD GOVERNMENT**
A detail (Palazzo Pubblico, Siena).

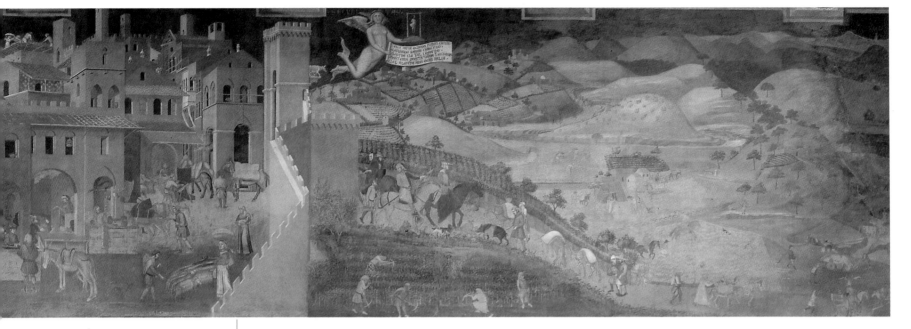

♦ **THE EFFECTS OF GOOD GOVERNMENT**
Ambrogio Lorenzetti, fresco, 1338-40 (Palazzo Pubblico, Siena). This painting is part of a fresco cycle entitled *The effects of Good and Bad Government in city and country.*

Ambrogio began to paint it in 1338 and it was probably finished in 1340. The frescos representing Good and Bad Government appear alternately around the walls. They include allegorical figures symbolizing the contrasting styles of government and precisely detailed realistic scenes of town and country life. The scenes illustrating *The effects of Good Government* show men and women busily engaged in the tasks of everyday life. In *The effects of Bad Government,* the city is shown in the grip of corruption, and the countryside is abandoned and desolate.

These scenes were evidently inspired by the townscape of Siena and the countryside surrounding it: on the one hand, the city can be recognized by its buildings and walls; and on the other, the undulating hills with vineyards and olive groves are typical of the area.

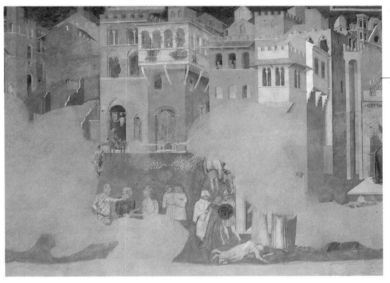

♦ **EFFECTS OF BAD GOVERNMENT**
A detail of the fresco in the Palazzo Pubblico.

♦ **EFFECTS OF BAD GOVERNMENT**
A detail of the fresco in the Palazzo Pubblico.

♦ **PIAZZA DEL CAMPO**
The outer edge is surrounded by tall buildings, from which the square slopes down to the Palazzo Pubblico, creating the impression of a vast stage set. The overall shape is that of a scallop shell, but it has also been compared to the Madonna's sheltering cloak. Reverence for Mary has always been strong in Siena, which takes pride in being known as the city of the Virgin.

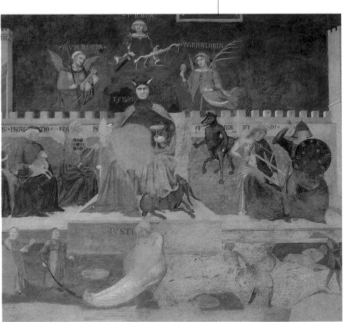

# ◆ KEY DATES IN GIOTTO'S LIFE

**1267** — Giotto born at Colle di Vespignano, in the Mugello area outside Florence. The name is a diminutive of Angelo, Angiolotto or Biagio. His father, Bondone, is a farmer and keeps sheep.

**1280** — Around this time, Giotto begins his apprenticeship as a painter at the workshop of Cimabue, who is the most successful artist in Florence at this time. Giotto travels a good deal with Cimabue and, when the master is invited to decorate the basilica of St Francis in Assisi, he is among his team of assistants.

**1287** — Marries Ciuta, short for Ricevuta, who over the years bears him eight children. Some follow in their father's footsteps but never attain the same artistic mastery.

**1290** — Begins painting his fresco cycle of the life of St Francis on the walls of the Upper Church in Assisi. Assisted by a team of collaborators, to whom he entrusts the preparatory work and the actual execution of his plans, he manages to finish the great task in five years.

**1300** — In Rome for the jubilee. It is probable that he visited the city several times while working at Assisi, wanting to familiarize himself with classical painting and the work of Pietro Cavallini, whom some scholars believe to have been his teacher. On this occasion, he has a commission from Boniface VIII to paint a fresco for the loggia of St John Lateran. This is to depict the Pope instituting the jubilee year.

**1302** — Goes to Padua to paint frescos for the basilica of St Anthony and for the Scrovegni Chapel. This second work, commissioned by Enrico Scrovegni to atone for the sins of his father Reginaldo, a usurer, keeps Giotto occupied until 1306.

**1310** — According to some art historians, it is around this time that Giotto creates the Navicella mosaic for the entrance to the original basilica of St Peter in Rome, now replaced by the present building. This is, however, a matter of controversy, and the mosaic may have been executed ten or so years earlier.

**1315** — This is thought to be the year in which he begins work on frescos for the Bardi and Peruzzi chapels in the Florentine church of Santa Croce.

**1328** — At the invitation of Robert of Anjou, he sets out for Naples. Of the many works by Giotto in that city, only a few fragments have survived.

**1334** — By public decree, he is appointed architect of Florence's city walls and superintendent of the work on Santa Reparata, the city's cathedral. The foundations of the bell tower he has designed are laid on 18 July, but he does not live to see it completed. Shortly after, he is called to Milan by the city's ruler, Azzo Visconti. No works survive from this period, but Giotto's influence is evident in the style adopted by contemporary painters living in the region.

**1337** — Giotto dies in Florence on 8 January and is buried with full honours in Santa Reparata.

# ◆ WHERE TO SEE WORKS BY GIOTTO

(Works marked "attr." have been attributed to Giotto, but not all art historians agree that he is the artist.)

## BRITAIN

**LONDON**
Private collection: *Redeemer in the act of blessing*, tempera on panel, 81 x 86 cm (32 x 34 in.) [attr.]
**OXFORD**
Ashmolean Musuem: *Madonna and child*, tempera on panel, 33 x 24 cm (13 x 9.5 in.) [attr.]

## FRANCE

**CHABLIS**
Musée Jacquemart-André: *St John the evangelist*, tempera on panel, 81 x 55 cm (32 x 22 in.) [attr.]; *St Lawrence*, tempera on panel, 81 x 55 cm (32 x 22 in.) [attr.]
**PARIS**
Louvre: *St Francis receiving the stigmata*, tempera on panel, 314 x 162 cm (124 x 64 in.) (originally from the church of St Francis in Pisa); *Crucifix*, tempera on panel, 277 x 225 cm (109 x 89 in.) [attr.]
**STRASBOURG**
Musées Municipaux: *Crucifixion*, tempera on panel, 39 x 26 cm (15 x 10 in.) [attr.]

## GERMANY

**BERLIN**
Staatliche Museen, Gemäldegalerie: *Crucifixion*, tempera on panel, 58 x 33 cm (23 x 13 in.); *Dormitio Virginis*, tempera on panel, 75 x 178 cm (29.5 x 70 in.)
**MUNICH**
Alte Pinakothek: *Last supper*, tempera on panel, 42.4 x 43 cm (17 x 17 in.); *Crucifixion*, tempera on panel, 45 x 43.5 cm (18 x 17 in.); *Descent into limbo*, tempera on panel, 45 x 44 cm (18 x 17 in.)

## HUNGARY

**BUDAPEST**
Szepmuvesvezeti Muzeum: *Allegorical figure of a woman*, fresco fragment, 27 x 15.5 cm (11 x 6 in.) [attr.]

## ITALY

**ASSISI**
Lower Church of St Francis: *Stories of St Nicholas* and *Stories of Lazarus and Mary Magdalene*, frescos [attr.]; *Six stories from the childhood of Christ*, frescos; *St Francis presents a skeleton*, fresco; *Christ in the act of blessing*, fresco; *Allegories of St Francis*, frescos
Upper Church of St. Francis: *Ceiling with doctors of the church*, frescos [attr.]; *Stories from the life of St Francis*, frescos
Eredi Fiumi Collection: *Saints Peter and Paul*, detached fresco
Pinacoteca comunale: *Maestà civica*, detached fresco, 350 x 160 cm (38 x 63 in.) [attr.]
**BOLOGNA**
Pinacoteca nazionale: *Bologna polyptych*, tempera on panel, 91 x 340 cm (36 x 134 in.)
**BORGO SAN LORENZO (FLORENCE)**
Pieve: *Madonna*, tempera on panel, 81.5 x 41 cm (32 x 16 in.)
**BOVILLE ERNICA (FROSINONE)**
San Pietro Ispano: *Angel*, mosaic, diameter 64 cm (25 in.)
**FLORENCE**
Berenson Collection (Villa i Tatti, Settignano): *St Anthony*, tempera on panel, 54 x 39 cm (21 x 15 in.) [attr.]; *Deposition*, tempera on panel, 44.5 x 43 cm (17.5 x 17 in.) [attr.]
Museo del Bargello: *Last Judgement, Stories of Mary Magdalene and John the Baptist*, frescos [attr.]
Museo Horne: *St Stephen*, tempera on panel, 84 x 54 cm (33 x 21 in.) [attr.]
Museo dell'Opera del Duomo: *Madonna and child* (recto), *Annunciation* (verso), tempera on panel, 94 x 42 cm (37 x 16.5 in.) [attr.]
Museo dell'Opera di Santa Croce: *Grieving Madonna*, detached fresco, 64 x 45 cm (25 x 18 in.) [attr.]
San Felice in Piazza: *Crucifix*, tempera on panel, 343 x 432 cm (135 x 170 in.) [attr.]
Santa Croce, Peruzzi chapel: *Stories of St John the Baptist and St John the Evangelist*, tempera on plaster; *Baroncelli polyptych*, tempera on panel, 185 x 323 cm (73 x 127 in.); Bardi chapel: *Stories of St Francis*, frescos
Santa Maria Novella: *Crucifix*, tempera on panel, 578 x 406 cm (227.5 x 160 in.)
Uffizi: *Enthroned Madonna and child*, tempera on panel, 180 x 90 cm (71 x 35 in.); *Madonna in majesty*, tempera on panel, 325 x 204 cm (128 x 80 in.); *Badia polyptych*, tempera on panel, 90 x 340 cm (35 x 134 in.) (originally from the Florentine church of the Badia)
**PADUA**
Basilica of St Anthony, chapter room: *St Francis receiving the stigmata, Martyrdom of Franciscans at Ceuta, Crucifixion, Heads of prophets*, fresco fragments
Scrovegni Chapel: *Stories from the life of Joachim, the Virgin Mary and Christ, Last Judgement, Allegories of Vices and Virtues*, frescos
Museo civico: *Crucifix*, tempera on panel, 223 x 164 cm (88 x 65 in.)
**RIMINI**
San Francesco (Tempio Malatestiano): *Crucifix*, tempera on panel, 430 x 303 cm (169 x 119 in.)
**ROME**
Museo Petriano: *Angel*, mosaic, diameter 65 cm (25.5 in.)
Pinacoteca Vaticana: *Stefaneschi polyptych*, tempera on panel, 220 x 245 cm (87 x 96 in.)
St John Lateran: *Boniface VIII instituting the jubilee*, fresco, 110 x 110 cm (43 x 43 in.)
Santa Maria Maggiore: shields with *The Eternal one in the act of blessing, Busts of prophets* and *The mystic lamb*, fresco fragments [attr.]

## UNITED STATES

**BOSTON**
Gardner Museum: *Presentation of Jesus in the temple*, tempera on panel [attr.]
**NEW YORK**
Wildenstein Collection: *Enthroned Madonna and child*, tempera on panel, 34.5 x 25.5 cm (13.5 x 10 in.) [attr.]
**RALEIGH (NORTH CAROLINA)**
Museum of Art: *Peruzzi polyptych*, tempera on panel, 667 x 217 cm (263 x 85 in.) [attr.]
**SAN DIEGO (CALIFORNIA)**
Fine Arts Gallery: *The Eternal one with angels*, cuspidate panel
**WASHINGTON**
National Gallery of Art: *Madonna and child*, tempera on panel, 85.5 x 62 cm (34 x 24 in.) [attr.]

# ◆ LIST OF WORKS INCLUDED IN THIS BOOK

N.B. Works of art of which only a detail is reproduced are marked D.

The works reproduced in this book are listed here with their date (when known), the place where they are currently housed, and the page number. The numbers in bold type refer to the credits on page 64. Abbreviations: UC, Upper Church of St Francis (Assisi); LC, Lower Church of St Francis (Assisi); SC, Scrovegni Chapel (Padua).

# ◆ INDEX

# ◆ CREDITS

The original and previously unpublished illustrations in this book may be reproduced only with the prior permission of Donati Giudici Associati, who hold the copyright.
The illustrations are by: Sergio (pp.4-5; 14-15; 16-17; 18-19; 20-21; 26-27; 30-31; 32-33; 34-35; 44-45); Andrea Ricciardi (pp.12-13; 15; 22; 28-29; 42-43; 54-55); Claudia Saraceni (pp. 12; 23; 42; 54); Giuseppe Arrighi (pp. 60-61); Alessandro Bartoloni (pp.8-9; 13); Roberto Lari (p.28); Francesco Lo Bello (p.6).
DOGI (ANTONIO QUATTRONE): 102; 104; 108.
DOGI (MARIO QUATTRONE): 17; 23; 26; 27; 28; 29; 30; 32; 34; 36; 37; 38; 39; 40; 41; 42; 43; 44; 45; 46; 47; 48; 49; 50; 51; 52; 53; 54; 55; 56; 57; 58; 59; 60; 61; 62; 63; 64; 65; 66; 67; 68; 69; 70; 71; 72; 73; 74; 75; 76; 77; 78; 80; 81; 82; 83; 84; 85; 86; 87; 89;

90; 91; 92; 93; 94; 95; 104; the photographs on page 9: church of St Francis and Orvieto cathedral; page 23: façade of Santa Maria Novella, Florence; page 36: interior of the Upper Church of St Francis, Assisi; page 48: views of the entrance wall and altar of the Scrovegni Chapel, Padua; page 57: façade of the church of Santa Croce, Florence, and the Baroncelli chapel.
ARCHIVIO ELECTA, Milan: 1; 2; 10; 16; 18; 20; 100 and the photographs on pages 8-9 of the cathedrals of Burgos, Exeter, Edinburgh, Amiens, Paris, Bamberg and Bonn.
ARCHIVIO FRANCO COSIMO PANINI, MODENA: 15; 31; 101; 105; 111; 112.
BIBLIOTECA NAZIONALE FLORENCE: 3.
BIBLIOTHEQUE NATIONALE, PARIS: 5.

CAPITOLINE LIBRARY, MODENA: 1.
FOTOARCHIVIO TODINI: 79.
GALLERIA NAZIONALE DELL'UMBRIA: 117.
PHOTO SCALA, FLORENCE: 6; 8; 9; 11; 12; 13; 14; 18; 19; 21; 24; 25; 35; 88; 96; 97; 98; 99; 118; 119; 120; and the photograph on page 7: interior of the church of Sant'Apollinare in Classe, Ravenna.
**Cover:** photographs from DoGi (Mario Quattrone); illustrations by Sergio.
**Title page** illustration: Sergio.

DoGi s.r.l. have made every effort to trace other possible copyright holders. If any omissions have been made, this will be corrected at reprint.